AF725722

THE LONG UNRAVELLING

THE LONG UNRAVELLING

What History Teaches Us About
Living Through Collapse

Racquel Hines Lynch

RHL Writes

THE LONG UNRAVELLING

What History Teaches Us About Living Through Collapse

Copyright © 2026 Racquel Hines Lynch

All rights reserved. No part of this book may be reproduced, stored in a retrieval system, or transmitted in any form or by any means, electronic, mechanical, photocopying, recording, or otherwise, without the prior written permission of the publisher, except in the case of brief quotations embodied in critical articles and reviews.

First edition, 2026

ISBN: 978-1-7647714-0-5 (paperback)

Published by RHL Writes

rhlwrites.com

Set in EB Garamond

Interior design and typesetting by RHL Writes

Cover design by RHL Writes

For my sons and grandsons, for whom I do all.

CONTENTS

INTRODUCTION

History Doesn't Repeat, But Human Nature Does

Every civilization believes it is permanent, and the belief endures right up until the point at which it cannot. This is not because people are foolish, but because decline, viewed from the inside, is almost impossible to see in real time. It arrives without announcement, as a slow accumulation of adjustments, inconveniences, and new normals that somehow never quite normalize, each one absorbed into ordinary life before its meaning has time to surface. The Roman senator watching barbarian migrations in the fourth century did not think he was witnessing the end of Rome; he thought he was managing a difficult period. The British financier in 1913 did not imagine the empire would fracture within a generation; he thought the fundamentals were sound. The American executive in 2007 did not see the housing collapse coming, even as the foundations trembled beneath his feet. In each case, the people living through decline experienced it not as catastrophe but as routine, and that is how civilizations have always experienced their own unravelling, less as drama than as the gradual accumulation of ordinary days.

Our relationship with historical patterns is a peculiar one. We study them carefully, teach them in schools, reference them in political speeches, and then proceed to ignore them almost completely when they begin to appear in our own time. The strangeness of this is not best explained by ignorance, but by something more fundamental in human psychology: we are pattern-recognition creatures who become selectively blind to patterns when we are living inside them, and the distance required to see a moment clearly is the one form of distance we cannot have about our own. The patterns persist anyway. Collapse rarely arrives as a single event; it tends to come slowly, silently, and ordinarily, surfacing first as a fraying of trust, a dull ache in the social fabric, a growing sense that the rules no longer quite work the way they once did. People stop noticing the fraying because each day feels remarkably like the one before, and by the time the history books are written the decline appears inevitable, even obvious, though to those who actually lived through it the experience registered mostly as tiredness.

We are living through such a moment now, and the signs are not subtle once one knows what to look for. Wealth concentrates at levels not seen since the Gilded Age, institutional distrust echoes the late Roman period, environmental limits press against a growth model that cannot acknowledge limits, and a pervasive sense among ordinary people suggests that the system is no longer working for them even as it claims to be functioning well. Yet most of us wake each morning, move through our routines, and assume tomorrow will be much like today. We adapt and adjust, calling it resilience when the more accurate word might be exhaustion.

The questions this book explores are not new. They have been asked in Athens and Alexandria, in Renaissance Florence and Revolutionary France, in Weimar Germany and post-industrial Detroit. What happens when growth stops being possible? How do societies respond when progress becomes a memory rather than a promise? What endures when the systems we have built around us begin to fail? And perhaps most urgently, what does it mean to live with clarity and integrity inside a system that is visibly coming apart? We have been here before, in different forms, under different names. Empires, markets, ideologies have all run the same course of growth, denial, decline, and renewal, and although the specifics change with each iteration, the underlying dynamics remain consistent enough that studying them is not an academic exercise so much as a form of practical preparation.

This is not a book of predictions. The future is always uncertain, always contingent on choices not yet made, and what this book offers instead is recognition, the capacity to see the cycles that history reveals so that we can respond to our moment honestly rather than with the mixture of denial and outrage that tends to characterise societies in decline. The aim is not fatalism, nor surrender to inevitability, but the clearer-eyed understanding that becomes available once we stop treating our own circumstances as exceptional.

The six lessons gathered here come from careful observation of how societies navigate turning points, drawing on economic history, psychological research, and the accumulated experience of people who have lived through collapse and renewal before. Some of what follows will be uncomfortable, because these lessons challenge assumptions that most of us have internalized so deeply we no longer recognize them as assumptions, treating them instead as facts about the world rather than as stories we have chosen to tell. Discomfort, in this kind of inquiry, is often the price of clarity.

The first lesson examines how progress transforms from tool to theology, tracing how every civilization eventually sanctifies its own success until questioning growth becomes a kind of heresy. The second explores the arithmetic of infinite growth mythology and what happens when material limits finally assert themselves, as they always do. The third traces the middle class as historical accident rather than natural order, and considers what its erosion means for social stability. The fourth looks at the psychology of living through decline, and at why collapse is so rarely recognized in real time by those experiencing it. The fifth asks what actually survives when systems fail. The sixth, which is perhaps the most personal, asks how we live well inside all of this, attending less to the question of how we might escape the long unravelling than to the question of how we move through it with our humanity intact.

Throughout these chapters, we will see how current events echo earlier crises, not because history repeats exactly, but because human beings respond to similar pressures in similar ways. We build, and then we overreach. We tell ourselves stories that justify what we want to believe. We ignore early warnings because acknowledging them would require us to change. And eventually, we reckon with realities we have been postponing for far longer than we should have.

What distinguishes our moment from some previous collapses is that we have the historical record. We can study what worked and what failed. We can recognise the early warning signs that previous generations missed or dismissed. We have, at least, the possibility of learning from the cycle rather than simply repeating it, and whether we exercise that possibility remains to be seen, although understanding the patterns is the necessary first step. With that in mind, we can begin where great unravelings tend to begin: with the stories a civilization tells itself about why it deserves its success, and with what happens, slowly at first and then all at once, when those stories stop being true.

Chapter One

When Progress Becomes Religion

The Sacred Story of More

Every empire sanctifies its own success, and this is less an act of cynicism than one of pattern recognition. Rome called it Pax Romana and divine mandate. The medieval Church called it God's will. The British Empire called it the civilising mission. The Soviet Union called it historical materialism and the inevitable march toward communism. We call it innovation, disruption, and the rising tide that lifts all boats. The specific theology shifts with each age, but the underlying mechanism remains consistent: societies that achieve material success develop elaborate explanatory frameworks that transform contingent advantages into moral imperatives, so that what begins as an honest acknowledgement that "we got lucky with geography and timing" evolves over time into "we are inherently superior," and finally crystallises into the position that to question our system is to question goodness itself.

This transformation is neither conspiracy nor conscious design. It is an emergent property of how human societies process success, expressing something fundamental about us as story-making creatures who need our circumstances to mean something. When we find ourselves on top, the easiest and most psychologically satisfying story to tell is that we have arrived there because we deserve to be there, and the closer we look at the historical record, the more consistently this pattern reveals itself.

Consider the American narrative of the twentieth century. In 1945, the United States emerged from World War II with its industrial base intact while much of Europe and Asia lay in ruins, a circumstance that produced an enormous but fundamentally temporary advantage. American factories could produce for the world, American workers could command high wages, and American corporations could dominate global markets, all of it traceable to the specific historical accident of being the only major industrial economy that had not been bombed. Within a generation, however, this contingent situation had been transformed in the national imagination into something essential about American character itself. The country was no longer understood to be successful because Europe was rebuilding and Japan was under occupation; it was understood to be successful because of its values, its hard work, its innovation, its freedom, its entrepreneurial spirit. The American Dream ceased to be a product of specific historical circumstances and became, in the telling, a reflection of American exceptionalism.

The reframing carried profound consequences. When the underlying circumstances inevitably changed, as Europe rebuilt, as Asian economies industrialised, as global competition returned, the response was not to adapt to new realities but to assume that if the old formulas were no longer working, they were simply not being applied vigorously enough. More deregulation, more tax cuts, more innovation, more freedom, always more. Progress, which had begun life as a tool for improving material conditions, had matured into an article of faith, and like all articles of faith it grew increasingly disconnected from the empirical reality it claimed to describe.

The Architecture of Inevitability

Walk through any major city in the developed world and you will see the physical manifestation of progress theology rising into the skyline. Glass towers climb upward, cranes turn in perpetual motion, and construction sites multiply across districts that were complete only a few years earlier, the architecture itself preaching a continuous sermon that upward is forward, that bigger is better, that the new is necessary by virtue of being new. This is not unique to our moment. Every civilisation encodes its values in its built environment. Rome covered the Mediterranean in roads and aqueducts that served as physical proof of imperial reach. Medieval Europe built cathedrals over generations as stone prayers pointing toward heaven. The industrial revolution erected factories and railway stations as temples to production and movement, monuments to the new theology of progress through mechanism.

Our era has introduced a particular and consequential innovation into this long tradition: we have built environments that require continuous growth simply to maintain themselves. The modern suburb sprawls across former farmland, dependent on cheap fuel and an expanding highway system to remain viable. The shopping mall is designed to maximise foot traffic and impulse purchasing rather than to function as a stable community space. The office park, the distribution centre, the data centre, each is predicated on the assumption that whatever they support will continue to expand indefinitely into the future. The result is a kind of architectural lock-in, in which anything less than growth begins to feel like failure: a stable population reads as stagnation, a steady-state economy reads as recession, and the infrastructure itself quietly demands that tomorrow be larger than today.

The psychological effects of this built environment are subtle but pervasive. When a daily commute moves past construction sites and development projects, when the skyline of one's city is perpetually changing, when the shop visited last year has been replaced by something newer this year, the message internalises itself without ever needing to be stated: this is what normal looks like, this is what progress means, and anything else can only be understood as decay. What the architecture does not reveal is the simpler truth that every growth curve eventually plateaus and every expansion eventually meets the limits that bounded it from the beginning, leaving open the slower and more difficult question of whether we will be able to recognise the plateau when it arrives, or whether we will experience it instead as the floor giving way beneath us.

When the Frontier Closes

The philosopher William James once observed that the most important events in human history are often unnoticed at the time they occur, and the closing of frontiers belongs firmly to that category of invisible watershed. For most of American history, there was somewhere else to go: land to settle, resources to extract, markets to open. This was not unique to America. Every expanding empire passes through a frontier phase during which growth seems limitless because limits have not yet been reached. The Roman frontier was the Mediterranean basin and then the lands beyond it. The British frontier was global, stretching from Bengal to the Cape. The American frontier was first continental, then hemispheric, and eventually financial, each redefinition stretching the concept further from its original geographic meaning.

Frontiers do close, however, and geography does run out. By 1890, the US Census Bureau had declared the American frontier officially closed, noting that there was no longer a clear line between settled and unsettled territory. This was a profound psychological shift even if most people living through it did not consciously register it as such, because the safety valve that an open frontier had provided, the sense that one could always start over somewhere else, had quietly disappeared. The response, characteristically, was to redefine the frontier rather than to acknowledge its closure. If there was no more geographic frontier, there would be a technological one. If there was no more land to settle, there would be markets to create. If there was no more physical expansion, there would be financial expansion. The frontier became metaphorical, abstract, and notionally infinite, untethered from the material constraints that had previously given it shape.

It is at this point that progress theology becomes genuinely dangerous. When growth was constrained by physical reality, by how much land could be cleared, how many crops planted, how many goods manufactured, there were natural limits that provided continuous feedback to the system. Once growth becomes abstract, however, measured in stock prices, GDP figures, and quarterly earnings reports, those feedback mechanisms weaken considerably, and the appearance of growth can be maintained through financial engineering, debt expansion, and asset inflation long after the underlying economy has stopped actually growing. The pattern recurs throughout history with remarkable consistency. Late Rome did not expand its productive capacity; it debased its currency. Eighteenth-century France did not develop its economy; it borrowed against an imagined future until revolution arrived alongside the debt collectors. The 2008 financial crisis was, in this sense, a frontier closing, the unsustainable expansion of credit finally reaching the wall of material reality that the financial system had spent decades pretending did not exist. Each time the wall is reached, the response follows the same pattern of denial, redefinition, and renewed effort to keep the story of perpetual expansion alive a little longer, because admitting that growth might end is not simply an economic acknowledgement but a crisis of meaning that the theological framework cannot easily survive.

THE HERESY OF LIMITS

In 1972, a group of researchers at MIT published a book called *The Limits to Growth*. Using systems modelling, they projected that if current trends in population, industrialisation, pollution, food production, and resource depletion continued unchanged, the world would reach ecological and economic limits within a century. The response was swift and vitriolic. Economists attacked the methodology, politicians dismissed it as alarmism, industry groups funded counter-studies, and the fundamental message at the heart of the book, that infinite growth on a finite planet is mathematically impossible, was treated not as a technical finding but as a moral failing.

The hostility makes sense once one understands what limits represent within a progress theology. If there are genuine limits to growth, the entire structure of meaning is threatened. If we cannot promise our children that they will be wealthier than we are, the question of what story we tell instead becomes urgent and unanswered. If we cannot expand forever, the current distribution of wealth and power loses one of its central justifications. If more is not automatically better, the question of how to measure a life well lived returns to the foreground, and few contemporary societies are equipped to answer it. These are not abstract philosophical questions. They strike at the heart of how modern societies organise themselves, because our economic system requires growth to function not as a preference but as a structural necessity. Debt-based monetary systems require expansion in order to generate the money required to pay interest. Pension systems require investment returns to fund retirements. Social stability depends on the continuing promise that conditions will improve over time.

When an entire civilisation is built around the assumption of perpetual growth, anyone who questions that assumption becomes threatening in a way that has little to do with being correct or incorrect. The discomfort produced by such questioning is structural, and that is why discussions of limits produce such heat in the public sphere. The argument is rarely about climate science or resource economics in any technical sense, although those subjects matter enormously. The deeper argument concerns what it means to belong to a society that can no longer promise that tomorrow will be larger than today, whether we can construct meaning and purpose in a world of sufficiency rather than expansion, and whether we can tell our children a different story that does not require infinite more to justify finite now. History suggests we do not handle these transitions well. When growth slows, societies fracture, because the consensus that held during expansion, that everyone would eventually benefit, that the rising tide would lift all boats, breaks down when the tide stops rising. Prosperity becomes zero-sum, and one person's gain begins to be experienced as another person's loss, which is the point at which empires become brittle and progress theology gives way to scapegoating and internal conflict.

The Temples We Build to Efficiency

Drive through any major industrial zone and you will see them: massive distribution centres, windowless and anonymous, stretching across what was recently farmland. Inside, algorithms optimise every movement, every route, every minute of human labour, and this is the temple of our particular moment, the place where contemporary civilisation worships at the altar of efficiency. Efficiency is not itself new, of course. Every civilisation has sought to do more with less. Our era has done something more particular, which is to make efficiency into a substitute for purpose. When we can no longer promise growth in living standards, we promise growth in productivity. When we cannot offer people meaningful work, we offer optimised work. When we cannot deliver genuine progress, we deliver progress theatre, the appearance of forward motion produced by ever more sophisticated measurement of activity that has lost its connection to underlying purpose.

Amazon warehouses are perhaps the purest expression of this dynamic, although they are far from the only one. Workers are tracked by algorithm, their movements measured to the second, their bathroom breaks timed, their walking routes calculated, their performance metrics updated continuously. The system is extraordinarily efficient at moving packages, and it is also extraordinarily efficient at eroding the dignity of the human beings inside it. This is not a criticism unique to one company. It is a pattern visible across the contemporary economy, in which efficiency has become an end in itself rather than a means to an end, and the obvious question has fallen out of the conversation entirely: efficient toward what purpose, productive of what kind of life?

The economist John Maynard Keynes predicted in 1930 that by the early twenty-first century, technological progress would allow people to work fifteen-hour weeks. We would have solved the problem of production, he argued, and could finally turn our attention to the problem of living well. He was half right. We did solve production, in the sense that material abundance is now technically achievable for everyone on the planet, but rather than working less we invented new forms of labour, new things to produce, new efficiencies to pursue, in part because the alternative would have required us to confront the question of what all of this productive capacity was actually for. The temples to efficiency reveal something important about our current moment in this respect. We have confused means and ends in a way that is difficult to see from inside the confusion. Progress was supposed to be about creating better lives, but somewhere along the way the creation of better lives became reframed as a matter of enabling more progress, the tool became the purpose, and the means became the end. A progress theology has fully matured when questioning the value of another marginal efficiency gain sounds like questioning goodness itself, when suggesting that people might work less and live more sounds radical rather than reasonable, and when proposing that we might optimise for human flourishing rather than GDP growth attracts the label of naivety or sentimentality.

When the Foundation Cracks

History teaches consistently that when a system can no longer tell the difference between growth and good, it is already in decline, and this is not a moral claim so much as one about feedback mechanisms. A healthy system maintains a connection between its instrumental goals, the making and moving and organising of things, and its ultimate purposes, which have to do with human welfare, social stability, and ecological sustainability. When the connection between instrumental and ultimate goals frays, the system begins optimising for metrics that have lost their meaning, continuing to function in measurable ways while drifting further from the purposes that justified its existence in the first place.

The pattern is visible across contemporary institutions. In education, test scores have largely replaced learning as the stated goal. In healthcare, treatment throughput has displaced healing. In media, engagement metrics have substituted for truth. In business, shareholder value has overtaken the broader stakeholder welfare that earlier generations of executives at least gestured toward. The metric becomes the mission, and the mission gets lost in the process of measuring it. Rome experienced a version of this when maintaining the army became more important than what the army was protecting. Medieval Catholicism experienced it when selling indulgences became more important than saving souls. Soviet communism experienced it when meeting production quotas became more important than producing useful goods. In each case, the system did not fail because it stopped being efficient at what it measured. It failed because what it measured had drifted away from what mattered, and the map and the territory eventually diverged so completely that the system could no longer find its way back to the ground that had originally given it meaning.

We are in that moment now, and the cracks are visible if one looks directly at them. Full-time workers cannot afford housing in the cities where they work. Stock markets reach record highs while life expectancy falls. Productivity continues to increase while wages stagnate. More stuff is produced and less satisfaction is felt. Children face worse material prospects than their parents despite higher education and harder work. These are not bugs in the system; they are signs that the system is functioning exactly as it has been designed to function, optimising for growth metrics that have lost their connection to human welfare. The foundation is not cracking under external pressure. It is cracking because it was built on assumptions that were always time-limited, and the time is running out faster than the architecture can be modified to accommodate the change.

The Question We Keep Avoiding

What we face, then, is a civilisation that has transformed progress from tool to theology, built its physical and social infrastructure around the assumption of perpetual growth, treated anyone who questions limits as heretical, worshipped efficiency while forgetting purpose, and optimised for metrics that have drifted away from meaning. The question of what happens next is one that history can illuminate without answering definitively, because it offers two broad patterns of response.

The first is denial followed by collapse followed by a prolonged period of reorganisation, during which the complexity and organisational capacity of the previous system is lost, living standards decline significantly, and cultural memory fragments. This is what happened to Rome's western empire over the course of several centuries. It is what nearly happened to Europe in the fourteenth century during the convergence of plague, famine, and social breakdown. It is what happened to many Indigenous civilisations after colonisation dismantled their existing systems faster than new ones could form to replace them.

The second pattern is adaptation, the painful but deliberate transition to a new organising story about what a society is for. This is what happened in Europe after the religious wars of the seventeenth century, when the theology of divine kingship slowly gave way to Enlightenment principles of reason and rights. It is what happened after World War II, when the theology of European empire gave way, however imperfectly, to frameworks of national self-determination and international cooperation. Such transitions are never clean, rarely peaceful, and involve profound disorientation as old certainties dissolve before new frameworks have had time to form, but they represent genuine transformation rather than simple collapse, and they reflect societies choosing, under pressure, to tell a different story about themselves than the one they had been telling.

The question facing us now is whether we can manage such a transition consciously, whether we can collectively recognise that progress theology has run its historical course and deliberately construct new stories about what makes life meaningful, what constitutes genuine success, and what we owe to each other and to the generations that will follow us, or whether we will cling instead to the old theology, insisting that we need only more growth, more efficiency, more innovation, until the foundation finally gives and we are forced to rebuild from what remains. History does not answer this question for us, but it does show us that the question has been faced before, that some societies have navigated it better than others, and that how a society responds during the period of recognition, before the crisis becomes undeniable to everyone, matters enormously for what comes after.

This is why the lesson comes first. Before we can usefully examine the fallacy of infinite growth, the dissolution of the middle class, the psychology of living through decline, or the question of what endures when systems fail, we need to understand the story that brought us here, seeing it clearly, without nostalgia and without contempt, as a story that served certain purposes for a certain period of time and has now reached the limits of what it can offer. The work of the chapters that follow rests on that recognition.

Chapter Two

The Fallacy of Infinite Growth

The Story That Shapes Everything

The myth of infinite growth is elegant and lethal, promising that if everyone keeps producing, consuming, and investing, everyone will eventually prosper. It suggests that economic expansion is not just possible but natural, the default state of a healthy civilisation, the direction history is meant to travel, and it transforms what should be a pragmatic question, how much is enough, into a moral imperative in which more is always better and wanting less becomes a failure of ambition or imagination. This is a lie in the deeper sense rather than the surface one, less a deliberate deception than a story that shapes reality even as it diverges from reality, a framework so thoroughly embedded in how we think that we cannot easily imagine thinking any other way.

Consider how completely growth logic has penetrated our language. A "healthy" economy is a growing economy. A "stagnant" economy is one that isn't growing, even if living standards are high and stable. "Recession" literally means a period of reduced economic activity, but we have come to treat it as near-catastrophic failure rather than as a normal cyclical adjustment. "Development" assumes movement toward more, never toward equilibrium. "Progress" points in one direction only. This linguistic framing is not neutral. It programmes us to see growth as natural and its absence as pathological, even though from almost any perspective outside modern economics the assumption is genuinely strange. Nature does not grow infinitely; it matures, stabilises, and cycles through periods of expansion and contraction. Human bodies do not grow infinitely; they develop to adulthood and maintain themselves through processes of regeneration rather than accumulation. Even mathematics recognises that exponential growth curves eventually hit limits and either plateau or collapse. Only in modern economics has infinite growth become the assumed baseline, and this assumption has reshaped how we organise society, measure success, and imagine the future, while quietly destroying the conditions that make civilisation possible.

The Arithmetic of Impossibility

The mathematics are inescapable, and they are the right place to start.

Compound growth is extraordinarily powerful. At a three percent annual growth rate, often cited as a healthy baseline for developed economies, an economy doubles in size every twenty-three years, so that an economy of a given size in 2000 would be twice that size by 2023, four times by 2046, eight times by 2069, and more than seventeen times its original size by the end of the century. Each doubling requires the same absolute increase in resource use as all previous growth combined. For most of economic history, this seemed manageable because economies were small relative to the planetary systems supporting them. There was always more forest to clear, more coal to mine, more oil to extract, more atmosphere available to absorb waste. The limits existed, but they were distant enough to seem theoretical, and theoretical limits exert almost no pressure on present behaviour.

Limits are never theoretical forever, however. They are only sometimes distant. We have reached the point at which economic activity has grown large relative to planetary boundaries, deforesting faster than forests can regenerate, extracting minerals faster than geological processes can replace them, emitting carbon faster than natural systems can absorb it, and generating waste faster than ecosystems can process it. The arithmetic is straightforward enough that it almost embarrasses to spell out: you cannot have infinite growth on a finite planet, something has to yield, either the growth or the planet, and since the planet's limits are physical rather than negotiable, it is the growth that will eventually give way to them.

Economists often respond to this argument with appeals to efficiency and innovation, suggesting that we will continue to grow by doing more with less, that we will dematerialise the economy through a shift from physical goods to digital services, that we will decouple growth from resource use through technological ingenuity. There is some truth in this. Efficiency has improved over time, and that improvement matters. The efficiency argument, however, has three structural problems that its proponents tend to understate. The first is Jevons' Paradox, named after the nineteenth-century economist William Stanley Jevons who first observed it in coal use. As steam engines became more efficient, total coal consumption increased, because the efficiency made coal-powered applications more economical and so more widespread. The same pattern recurs across resources and eras: more efficient cars produce more driving, more efficient electronics produce more devices, more efficient agriculture produces more food waste. Efficiency gains tend to expand consumption rather than reduce it, because they lower the cost of doing more. The second problem is thermodynamic. There are absolute physical limits to how efficient any process can be. You cannot create energy from nothing. You cannot eliminate waste entirely. At some point, efficiency improvements yield diminishing returns, and further growth requires more absolute resource use regardless of how cleverly that use is organised. The third problem is the most fundamental, which is that you cannot fully dematerialise an economy. Digital services still require physical infrastructure, including servers, networks, devices, and electricity generation. Even a highly dematerialised economy needs food, water, housing, transport, and healthcare, all of which have irreducible physical requirements. The economy is not an abstract mathematical system; it is embedded in the physical world, and the physical world has boundaries that do not move because we would prefer them to.

Three percent annual growth forever is mathematically impossible on a finite planet. Whether that impossibility manifests as ecological collapse, resource depletion, or social breakdown first is debatable. That it will manifest in some form is not.

When Frontiers Close, We Turn Inward

There is a historical pattern that follows from this arithmetic with considerable consistency: when external expansion becomes impossible, societies turn inward, and when they turn inward, the character of economic activity changes in ways that are recognisable across very different historical periods. During expansion, growth is extensive: you create more by using more, more resources, more territory, more people incorporated into the economic system, and the pie grows larger because you are drawing from a larger area. This is how growth worked during the colonial period, during the settlement of new continents, during the postwar globalisation of the mid-twentieth century. When new territory runs out, growth must become intensive: you extract more from the same space by optimising, financialising, and speculating. The pie cannot get physically larger, so it gets sliced differently, traded faster, made into derivatives, and eventually traded as claims on future slices that may never materialise.

This is what has been happening across most developed economies for the past four decades. Unable to expand the real economy at accustomed rates, capital has flowed increasingly into the financial economy. Complex financial instruments proliferate. Debt-fuelled consumption is encouraged. Asset prices are inflated through monetary policy. Speculation is treated as if it were production. The result is an economy that appears to be growing when measured in asset prices and financial aggregates, but feels like stagnation to the majority of people, because most of that growth is occurring in the financial sector, benefiting primarily those who already own financial assets, while wages stagnate and material conditions deteriorate for everyone else.

This is not a new pattern. Late Rome, unable to expand further, turned to currency debasement and the extraction of its own citizens through taxation. Late medieval Europe, when territorial expansion had exhausted itself, saw the growth of increasingly complex credit instruments and debt relationships. The Gilded Age followed the plateau of American industrial expansion with an explosion of financial speculation. The pattern repeats with remarkable consistency: extensive growth slows, intensive extraction increases, wealth concentrates, financial complexity expands, inequality spikes, and eventually the system reaches a crisis that forces restructuring. We are in the intensive extraction phase now. The frontiers are closed, the easy growth is over, and what we have instead is the sophisticated appearance of growth, financial engineering presented as economic vitality, asset inflation presented as prosperity, speculation presented as investment.

The Great Speculation

Walk through any major financial district and you will see the physical expression of this shift, in the glass towers housing trading floors where algorithms execute millions of transactions per second, the conference rooms where derivatives are structured and priced, the offices where wealth managers help the already-wealthy navigate tax arrangements while generating returns from instruments most people cannot explain let alone access. This is where the modern economy largely happens, at least as measured by GDP. In the United States, finance accounts for nearly a quarter of economic output, manufacturing accounts for roughly fifteen percent, and agriculture less than one percent, which means that the most economically dominant nation in the world makes most of its measured money by moving money around.

The fundamental shift began in the 1970s and accelerated through the decades that followed. As profit rates in manufacturing and industry declined, a natural consequence of market maturation and the emergence of global competition, capital flowed toward financial activity, because money could be made not by building things but by trading them, by creating financial instruments, by arbitrage and speculation. The barrier to entry was low if you had capital, the returns were high, and the social justification was thin but sufficient: markets were said to be allocating capital efficiently toward its highest use. This required a cultural shift as well as an economic one. Speculation, which had been viewed with suspicion through most of the twentieth century and was subject to significant regulatory constraint after the Depression, became respectable again. Financial traders became celebrated figures. The proposition that making money from money was not just acceptable but the highest form of economic sophistication embedded itself into business culture and policy alike.

The consequences appeared in compensation data. In the mid-1960s, chief executives in the United States earned roughly twenty times the pay of average workers, and by 2020 that ratio exceeded 350 to one. This did not reflect a 350-fold increase in executive productivity or contribution. It reflected the fact that compensation had shifted toward stock options and financial instruments, and those instruments had appreciated dramatically as the financial economy expanded well beyond the real economy it was nominally serving. Private equity, hedge funds, and venture capital followed the same logic at scale. These entities do not primarily create new businesses or products. They extract value from existing enterprises through financial engineering, acquiring companies, loading them with debt, stripping assets, reducing workforces, and selling at profit, transferring wealth from workers and communities to investors, from future stability to present returns, from stakeholders to shareholders. When you can no longer grow the pie, you fight over how it is sliced, and in that fight those who control capital have structural advantages, including the capacity to shape regulation in their favour, to move money across borders to minimise taxation, and to structure transactions that extract value while offloading risk onto workers, consumers, and governments. They can, in effect, harvest the accumulated value of institutions and communities faster than those institutions and communities can replace it.

The great speculation is not primarily about stock markets, though markets are part of it. It is about an entire economy that increasingly measures success in financial abstractions rather than in material improvements to human welfare, that rewards extraction over creation, speculation over production, financial engineering over the kind that produces actual things. This is ultimately unsustainable, not as moral critique but as observation, because you cannot eat stock certificates or shelter in derivatives, and when the financial economy grows sufficiently disconnected from the real economy, reality reasserts itself, as it always has and always does.

The Ecology of Depletion

Return now to the physical world, because that is ultimately where all economic activity occurs and where all limits are finally encountered. The story of modern economic growth is, in material terms, the story of fossil fuels. Everything we associate with industrial civilisation changed when coal and then oil became widely accessible, because for the first time in human history civilisation had access to energy that did not depend on current solar input. We could burn the concentrated sunshine of millions of years of geological time, which was, in effect, the discovery of an enormous energy inheritance that we have been spending for roughly two centuries. That inheritance enabled what we call progress: industrialisation, mechanisation, the transformation of agriculture, global transportation networks, and the digital age. All of it runs on fossil energy, either directly or embedded in the production processes that make it possible, and even renewable energy infrastructure requires fossil fuels to manufacture, since solar panels involve coal-powered smelting, rare earth minerals, and petroleum-derived materials in their production.

The problems this creates are multiple. The most discussed is climate, the carbon released through fossil fuel combustion warming the planet at a rate unprecedented in human civilisation, although this is not only an environmental problem but an economic one, since climate change damages agriculture, disrupts supply chains, destroys infrastructure, forces migration, and generates conflict. These are not future costs being incurred for future people. They are current costs, growing in scale, being paid now by communities that in many cases contributed least to creating them. Less discussed but equally significant is the broader pattern of resource depletion. Topsoil is eroding faster than it is being created, a slow-motion threat to the agricultural systems that feed the world. Aquifers accumulated over geological timescales are being drawn down in decades.

Phosphorus, which is essential for agriculture and has no substitute, is being extracted from finite geological deposits with no plan for what follows depletion. Ocean fisheries that sustained human populations for millennia are collapsing under the pressure of industrial-scale extraction.

None of this appears in standard GDP calculations. Cutting down a forest registers as economic activity. Depleting an aquifer registers as agricultural output. Even the costs of climate damage, the disaster recovery spending, the insurance losses, the emergency responses, register as GDP. Our primary measure of economic success is structurally blind to ecological degradation until that degradation becomes a crisis large enough to overwhelm the systems it has been undermining. This is the core problem with the growth paradigm: it treats a finite planet as an infinite resource base and an infinite waste sink, draws down natural capital and accounts for it as income, and does this not through malice but through the logical operation of economic models that were designed for a world in which natural systems were so large relative to human activity that they could be treated as effectively boundless. That world no longer exists, and the question is not whether adaptation to a world of different limits will be required, because it will, but whether that adaptation happens consciously, equitably, and by design, or is imposed through the accumulating pressure of crises that might have been anticipated.

The Economics of Enough

If infinite growth is impossible and we are already pressing against various planetary boundaries, the natural question is what comes instead. The honest answer is that nobody knows exactly, and anyone who claims otherwise is selling something. What we can say with reasonable confidence is that the transition away from growth-dependent systems will require changes more fundamental than the adjustment of a few policy levers.

Consider how deeply growth is embedded in the monetary system. Most money in modern economies is created through bank lending. When a bank issues a loan, it creates new money, and that money must be repaid with interest. The money to pay the interest must come from somewhere, and in practice it comes from continued economic growth that generates enough new activity to service existing debt. In a genuinely steady-state economy, this mechanism breaks down: debt becomes harder to service, defaults accumulate, and the financial system, built on the assumption of perpetual expansion, becomes unstable. Or consider employment. Work has been organised around the assumption of continuous expansion, so that companies hire when growing and shed workers when growth slows, while healthcare, retirement security, and social identity have all been tied to employment in ways that make unemployment not just economically painful but personally destabilising. An economy that stops growing, within current institutional arrangements, produces unemployment and the social costs that follow it. Or consider pension and retirement systems, which are predicated on investment returns, which require growth, leaving an ageing population that has been promised retirement security based on a growth model that has run its course facing a structural problem that no amount of individual responsibility can resolve.

The alternative frameworks that economists working in this space have proposed share certain features. Money creation would need to be decoupled from lending, removing the structural requirement for continuous expansion. Work would need to be decoupled from income, through some combination of reduced working hours, universal basic services, and different forms of social provision. Success would need to be measured by indicators of genuine welfare, by health, education, ecological integrity, and social cohesion, rather than by aggregated output. Taxation would need to shift from income and labour toward resource use and wealth concentration. These proposals are not utopian in the sense of being impossible. They describe real policy choices that real governments could make. They are, however, politically difficult in proportion to how thoroughly the existing system has shaped both institutions and expectations, and the people who benefit most from current arrangements are also those with the most capacity to resist changing them.

What history suggests is that the transition to different economic arrangements tends not to happen through rational democratic deliberation in conditions of stability. It tends to happen through crisis. The New Deal was not passed because Americans had thoughtfully concluded that regulated capitalism was theoretically superior. It was passed because the Depression had made the previous arrangements intolerable. The postwar welfare state was not built because politicians had read the right economists. It was built because two world wars had made the social cost of ignoring ordinary people's welfare politically unsustainable. This does not mean we should wait for crisis. It means we should understand that the crisis may be doing more of the work than the argument, and plan accordingly.

What We Tell Ourselves

Here is the uncomfortable thing. Most people, at some level, already know that infinite growth is impossible. They know the current system is ecologically destructive. They know inequality is corroding social stability. They know something is being consumed that cannot be replaced. They also know that acknowledging this openly, and acting on it consistently, would require changes so profound that the prospect is genuinely overwhelming. It would mean reconsidering career choices and lifestyle assumptions. It would mean confronting the possibility that the life built around certain promises might be built on a premise that was always time-limited. It would mean asking questions about what we owe to people who do not yet exist, in a present that already demands enough from us.

So we engage in motivated reasoning. Technology will solve it. Efficiency will be sufficient. Someone else will work it out. It is not as bad as the pessimists suggest. The future is uncertain, so why act on projections. Change would be too expensive. Change would be too disruptive. These are not conscious lies. They are psychological defence mechanisms against an anxiety that, if fully felt, would be difficult to function alongside. They remain, however, at their core, a form of avoidance, and the longer the avoidance continues, the more constrained the eventual choices become.

History does not record a single case of physical limits disappearing because a civilisation needed them to. Limits do not become negotiable through optimism or political will. They yield, temporarily, to ingenuity and efficiency. They do not yield permanently to anything. Reality wins, and the only variable is the manner in which it wins, and whether the people navigating that moment have prepared themselves to respond with something more useful than surprise. The fallacy of infinite growth is not primarily an economic error. It is a story about meaning, one that answers the question of what makes a life or a society worth living with a single, endlessly deferred answer: more. Understanding why that story is false, and what might replace it, is not a technical problem but a human one, which is why no amount of economic modelling, on its own, will resolve it. That work belongs to the chapters that follow.

Chapter Three

The Middle Class Mirage

The Historical Accident We Called Normal

The middle class, that symbol of democratic stability, that aspiration of the capitalist promise, that presumed bulwark against political extremism, is not a natural feature of market economies. It is a historical accident, a brief equilibrium of forces that emerged under specific conditions, held for a few decades in a handful of countries, and is now dissolving as those conditions change. This matters enormously, because we have built our entire political and social narrative around the assumption that middle-class life is the default state of developed economies, that it emerges naturally from market operations, that it reflects timeless principles of hard work and merit rewarded, and none of this is true. Recognising it as untrue is essential to understanding both where we are and where the evidence suggests we are heading.

For most of economic history, societies were bifurcated. A small elite owned land or capital. A large population worked for subsistence. There was no broad middle. Medieval Europe had nobility and peasants. Ancient

Rome had patricians and plebeians. Agrarian societies everywhere had landlords and tenant farmers. The distribution was pyramid-shaped, with a vast base, a tiny peak, and minimal middle, and this was not because people did not want more secure lives but because the economics of pre-industrial societies did not generate the surplus required to sustain a large middle layer. The elite extracted what surplus existed, and everyone else lived close to subsistence.

The middle class emerged when a specific and unusual set of conditions aligned simultaneously. Industrialisation created demand for skilled labour. Unionisation created bargaining power for workers who would otherwise have had none. Wars created labour scarcity that temporarily shifted the balance between capital and labour. Postwar reconstruction created opportunity. Progressive taxation funded public infrastructure. Mass education systems created mobility. Regulation constrained the most predatory practices. Democratic politics gave workers a degree of political voice that their economic position alone would never have secured. In several developed economies, and most visibly in the United States, this alignment produced what is now remembered as the Golden Age of capitalism, the period from roughly 1945 to 1975, when worker productivity and wage growth tracked together, when single incomes could support families, when employer-provided pensions and healthcare were common, when home ownership expanded across class lines, and when each generation could reasonably expect to live materially better than the one before it.

The crucial recognition is that this was an aberration rather than a norm. It required a specific and temporary constellation of circumstances, including industrial dominance, strong unions, progressive taxation, regulated capitalism, limited financial speculation, and a political consensus that broadly shared prosperity was both desirable and achievable. It was constructed, deliberately and through conflict, rather than discovered as the natural operation of markets, and when the conditions that constructed it were dismantled, it dissolved. Not because of personal failures or cultural decline, but because the structural foundations that held it in place were removed. What we are returning to is closer to the historical norm: a society with concentrated wealth at the top and precarity for most people below it. This is not a tragic deviation from capitalism. It is what capitalism has looked like through most of its history, in the absence of the specific political constraints that briefly produced something different.

The Great Compression and Its Unravelling

Economists refer to the period from roughly 1930 to 1980 as the Great Compression, a period during which income inequality in the United States and other developed economies narrowed substantially from its Gilded Age peaks. The term is somewhat misleading, because it implies that something was compressed by external force rather than actively constructed through deliberate policy choices. What actually happened was a series of interventions that constrained capital and empowered labour over several decades. The New Deal in the 1930s created social security, unemployment insurance, labour protections, and financial regulation. The Second World War brought massive public investment, high taxation, and price controls alongside labour scarcity that strengthened workers' bargaining position. The postwar period maintained high marginal tax rates on top incomes, strong antitrust enforcement, and trade unions representing a substantial proportion of the workforce. Public investment in infrastructure, education, and housing created opportunity that was genuinely broad rather than concentrated.

These were not natural market outcomes. They were political choices, made in response to the accumulated lessons of catastrophe. The Gilded Age had ended in Progressive Era reforms that were subsequently rolled back in the 1920s, contributing to the conditions for the Great Depression. The Depression had generated fascism in Europe and serious socialist movements across the democratic world. The policymakers who built the postwar settlement understood, through direct experience, that extreme inequality breeds political instability, that concentrated wealth is incompatible with sustained democracy, and that capitalism without constraints tends toward the conditions that had twice in a generation brought civilisation to the edge of collapse. So they built constraints, and for roughly four decades those constraints produced what they were designed to produce. The middle class expanded, inequality declined, living standards rose broadly, and democratic capitalism appeared, for a time, to have resolved its internal contradictions.

Beginning in the 1970s, the dismantling began. The intellectual justification was that regulation was stifling innovation, that unions were reducing competitiveness, that high taxes were discouraging investment, that government intervention was distorting the efficient operation of markets. The prescription was deregulation, the reduction of union power, tax cuts concentrated at the top, and reduced public spending. The promise was that liberating markets would generate growth so abundant that everyone would benefit through the mechanism of the rising tide. What the data shows is that growth continued, but it accrued almost entirely to those at the top. Worker productivity continued to rise, but wages stagnated. Corporate profits expanded, but labour's share of GDP declined. From 1948 to 1973, productivity and typical compensation grew in tandem, roughly doubling together. From 1973 to 2018, productivity increased by approximately seventy percent while typical worker compensation increased by roughly twelve percent. The tide rose. The boats at the bottom barely moved.

By the early 2020s, wealth inequality across developed economies had returned toward Gilded Age levels. The share of wealth held by the top one percent had grown dramatically while the share held by the bottom half had declined. Tens of millions of working adults could not cover a modest unexpected expense from their savings. Student debt had become a structural feature of young adult life rather than a manageable temporary burden. Medical costs were pushing significant numbers of households into financial crisis. Housing costs in many cities were consuming incomes at rates that made saving for security effectively impossible. The Great Compression had unravelled, and in its wake the middle class was hollowing out, contracting between a smaller group maintaining security and a larger group experiencing the downward mobility that the whole arrangement had been designed to prevent.

The Geography of Abandonment

The dissolution of the middle class is not only a matter of statistics. It has a physical geography, visible in the landscape of former industrial communities across the developed world. Drive through the Midwest of the United States, the former industrial heartlands of northern England, the peripheral regions of southern Europe, or the post-industrial towns of Australia's manufacturing regions, and you will see the same pattern written into the built environment. Towns organised around industries that no longer exist. Commercial centres with vacant premises. Housing stock declining in value. Infrastructure ageing without maintenance. Schools and public services underfunded. Social fabric stretched or broken.

This is not happening because people in these places stopped working hard or lost their values. It is happening because the economic model that sustained these communities, industrial employment providing stable wages, benefits, and retirement security, was dismantled in the name of efficiency and shareholder value. The factories closed not because of abstract market forces operating independently of human decisions, but because specific policy choices, including trade agreements that prioritised capital mobility over community stability, deregulation that removed constraints on corporate behaviour, and tax arrangements that rewarded offshoring, made it profitable to move production to lower-wage environments and extract the difference.

The result is what geographers call spatial inequality, which describes not simply income differences between individuals but the systematic disinvestment from entire regions. Capital concentrates in a small number of cities where it can generate the highest returns, while everywhere else experiences slow decline. This creates a self-reinforcing dynamic. As communities lose their economic base, younger people leave to find opportunity elsewhere. Population decline reduces the tax base. Public services deteriorate. Infrastructure ages. Social fabric weakens. The people who remain face rising costs alongside declining resources, and the resulting despair registers in declining life expectancy, rising rates of substance abuse and suicide, and the collapse of the social institutions, the clubs, churches, civic organisations, that once gave community life its texture. These are not random patterns. They are the predictable consequences of an economic system that extracts value from communities without reinvesting, that treats workers as disposable inputs rather than as stakeholders in shared prosperity, and that externalises the social costs of its decisions onto the people and places least able to absorb them.

The politics that emerge from these conditions follow a pattern that is also not new. When the system stops delivering for people who did what they were told, when the promises turn out to have been hollow, when the children face worse prospects than the parents despite working harder and acquiring more credentials, people become receptive to those who promise to blow up the existing arrangements. Populism, nationalism, and political extremism do not emerge from nowhere. They grow in the specific soil of broken promises, concentrated grievance, and the reasonable conclusion that the institutions promising fairness are not, in fact, delivering it. The pattern has played out in late Rome, in pre-revolutionary France, in the Gilded Age, and in the interwar period that preceded fascism, and although the specific forms differ across these episodes, the underlying dynamic of concentrated wealth, hollowed middle, and political crisis remains consistent.

The Professionalisation of Everything

The erosion of middle-class security is not confined to industrial communities. It is equally visible in the transformation of the professions, those occupations that for much of the twentieth century represented the most stable and secure form of middle-class life. Consider medicine. A generation ago in most developed countries, the majority of doctors worked in private practice or small partnerships. They controlled their working conditions, exercised professional autonomy, and were compensated well enough to sustain genuinely secure lives. Today, the majority work as employees of large health systems, hospital networks, or increasingly of private equity-owned practice groups, working longer hours under more bureaucratic constraint, with less autonomy over clinical decisions, higher administrative burdens, and compensation that, relative to the debt and training required to enter the profession, represents a significantly worse return than it once did. The profession is being converted, in economic terms, from autonomous practice into wage labour.

The pattern repeats in law, where partnership-track positions are declining and being replaced by contract and staff attorney roles, creating a bifurcated profession with a small elite earning very well and a large cohort in precarious employment. It repeats in academia, where tenure-track positions represent a shrinking proportion of teaching roles, with the majority now held by adjunct and casual staff working without job security, benefits, or wages that reflect the years of training required to do the work. It is visible in architecture, in journalism, in social work and counselling, and in engineering. The consistency of the pattern across such different fields suggests a common cause. Professional knowledge that once commanded market power is being systematically deskilled, standardised, and made substitutable through consolidation and technology. Ownership of professional practices is concentrating. What was once a relationship between a professional and their clients or patients is being intermediated by corporate structures whose primary obligation is to their investors. The professional class is discovering, several decades after the industrial working class made the same discovery, that the conditions which sustained their position were political and institutional rather than inherent to the nature of their work.

The practical consequence is that people who followed the prescribed path, acquired advanced credentials, chose recognised professions, and worked diligently, now find themselves on shakier ground than that path was supposed to guarantee. The promise of professional security as a reliable route to middle-class stability is dissolving even for those who believed in it most completely and fulfilled its requirements most faithfully.

When Fairness Fails

What holds societies together across their internal divisions is not primarily shared ethnicity, religion, or culture, though these play roles in different contexts. It is the belief, however imperfect, that the system distributes its rewards and burdens with something approximating fairness, that effort produces decent outcomes, that the rules apply to everyone, that the next generation has a reasonable prospect of doing better than the current one, and that power is not entirely unaccountable. When that belief erodes, when people conclude through their own experience that the game is structured in favour of those who already have the most, that effort and rule-following do not protect you while they do protect others, that opportunity is foreclosing rather than opening, social cohesion fails. Not dramatically, not all at once, but in the steady accumulation of disengagement, cynicism, and the withdrawal of the basic good faith that institutions require in order to function.

We are watching this happen. Declining trust in institutions, in governments, courts, media, and professional expertise, is not an irrational response to manipulation. It is, in large part, a rational response to the lived experience of systems that have systematically failed the people who needed them most while protecting and enriching those who needed protection least. If you did what the system asked of you and still cannot afford housing, medical care, or basic security, distrust is not a pathology but a form of pattern recognition. If you watch those responsible for catastrophic failures be rewarded rather than held accountable, scepticism about accountability is not cynicism but an evidence-based response.

The consequences of this erosion are also historically consistent. Rising authoritarianism as people seek strong leadership to cut through systems that seem broken. Increasing scapegoating as communities look for legible explanations for diffuse suffering. Growing political extremism as the moderate centre fails to deliver and loses credibility. The potential for violence as institutional channels for legitimate grievance are blocked or discredited. And eventually, a crisis that does not reform the system so much as shatter it and force the construction of something from the remains. We have seen this sequence in the collapse of the Roman Republic, in the revolutions of the eighteenth and nineteenth centuries, and in the political catastrophes of the 1930s. In each case the proximate causes differ, but the underlying structure remains the same: concentrated wealth, hollowed middle, eroded fairness, institutional failure, and political crisis.

What We Owe Each Other

The question of what fairness actually requires, not as moral philosophy but as practical necessity for sustaining civilisation, has a historically consistent answer. You need enough broadly shared prosperity to give most people a genuine stake in maintaining the existing arrangements. This does not mean equality of outcome. Hierarchies appear to be a persistent feature of human social organisation. It does mean that the distribution of resources cannot become so extreme that large populations experience nothing to gain from stability and nothing to lose from disorder.

The mid-twentieth century understanding of this requirement was codified in the concept of the social wage: the recognition that people needed not just market incomes but collective provision of healthcare, education, retirement security, and public infrastructure. Markets, left to themselves, would not provide these adequately or distribute them broadly enough to sustain social cohesion. Government therefore needed to ensure them, not as charity but as the investment required to maintain the social stability that everyone, including elites, depended on. This was not an idealistic position. It was a pragmatic one, arrived at through the experience of what happened when it was neglected. Elites who understood history grasped that their own security depended on broad social stability, and that broad social stability required that ordinary people have enough to feel invested in the continuation of the current order. High taxes and strong regulations were a price worth paying relative to the alternative that inequality, if left unchecked, reliably produced.

That understanding has since been replaced, across most developed economies, by the logic of individual responsibility, according to which if you are struggling it is because you made inadequate choices, lacked sufficient effort, or failed to develop the right skills. The system is not responsible for your outcomes. You are. This framing is both empirically inaccurate and socially destructive. It is inaccurate because individual outcomes are heavily determined by structural factors that individuals did not choose and cannot individually change, including where you were born, what resources your family had, what opportunities existed in your community, and what economic conditions prevailed when you entered the workforce. It is destructive because it converts collective failures into individual blame, making solidarity harder to sustain and collective action harder to legitimate.

What we owe each other, as a matter of practical social necessity rather than abstract ethics, is recognition that we exist in systems of mutual dependence. Elite prosperity depends on the labour and consumption of workers. Urban stability depends on the health of regional communities. The future depends on investment in the present. The rights of the powerful depend, ultimately, on the consent of those over whom power is exercised. None of what this requires is historically radical. Progressive taxation that prevents extreme wealth concentration, robust public investment in education and infrastructure, strong labour protections, universal provision of healthcare and retirement security, and regulation of capital sufficient to prevent the most extractive practices: this is the formula that produced the brief period of broad middle-class prosperity that many now remember as normal. The genuinely radical proposition is the current one, that stable democracy can be maintained while wealth concentrates at historically extreme levels, while communities hollow out, while opportunity forecloses, and while fairness becomes increasingly implausible as a description of how the system actually operates.

History does not support that proposition. Societies that stop believing in fairness do not simply become less equal. They become something more volatile, more susceptible to authoritarian promises, and ultimately less stable for everyone in them, including those at the top. The middle-class mirage matters not because middle-class life is inherently the best way to organise human existence, but because the conditions that produced a broad middle produced something else alongside it: a population with enough stake in the system to defend it, enough security to plan beyond immediate survival, and enough experience of genuine opportunity to believe that the rules of the game were worth following. Lose those conditions, and you lose more than a demographic category. You lose the social foundation that democratic politics requires in order to function. That foundation is eroding, and understanding how it was built and why it was dismantled is the necessary precondition for thinking seriously about what rebuilding it might require.

Chapter Four

The Psychology of Collapse

Why We Can't See What's Happening

Collapse is rarely recognised in real time because it does not feel like destruction. It feels like exhaustion. This may be the most important and least understood aspect of historical decline, the fact that decline is not dramatic but ordinary, that it presents itself as the slow accumulation of small breakdowns that people adapt to, normalise, and incorporate into their sense of how things work. The lights still come on. The shops still have food. The routines continue. Everything seems mostly manageable until, gradually and then suddenly, it isn't.

Psychologists have a name for this process. Shifting baseline syndrome describes the way each generation takes the conditions it grew up with as the standard for normal, even when those conditions represent significant degradation from what the previous generation experienced. The baseline shifts with each adaptation, and because no single adaptation is large enough to register as catastrophe, the cumulative deterioration goes unmeasured and often unnamed. Consider how this operates with economic decline. Real wages across much of the developed world have stagnated for decades while productivity has continued to rise, which means an entire working lifetime of not getting ahead despite working harder. Because it happens incrementally, because people find ways to cope, working longer hours, adding household earners, taking on debt, quietly lowering their expectations for what a decent life might look like, it does not feel like societal failure. It feels like a personal challenge that everyone else must somehow be handling better, and the structural nature of the problem is obscured by the individualisation of the experience.

This is the psychology of collapse: adaptation to degradation, normalisation of dysfunction, and the persistent confusion of adjustment with stability. We believe we are managing when we are actually declining. We experience the symptoms of systemic failure as personal inadequacy. By the time the breakdown becomes undeniable, the capacity to respond to it effectively has often already been quietly eroded.

The Crisis Is Ambient

Walk through any major city in the developed world and you will see things that would have been considered shocking a generation ago, now simply part of the landscape. Rough sleeping not as occasional misfortune but as a permanent feature of public space. People rationing medications or forgoing medical care because of cost. Infrastructure visibly ageing without maintenance. Public services contracted to the point where they fail the people who need them most. The accumulated evidence of systems that are not working, normalised into background noise. This is what ambient crisis looks like: ongoing emergency that has been adapted to rather than addressed.

The normalisation operates through a particular psychological mechanism, in which each individual failure is processed as a specific, bounded problem rather than as evidence of a pattern. Rough sleeping is a housing problem. Medical debt is a healthcare problem. Crumbling infrastructure is a budget problem. Declining life expectancy is a public health problem. Processed separately, each seems like a distinct policy failure with distinct solutions. Seen together, they are something else: the coordinated expression of systems that are failing across multiple domains simultaneously. We are not well-equipped, however, either psychologically or institutionally, to process that kind of systemic signal. Our attention is drawn to discrete events rather than to slow trends. Our media and political systems reward crisis response over crisis prevention. Our cognitive architecture is better suited to responding to visible, immediate threats than to recognising the slow convergence of diffuse ones. The result is what might be called the normalisation of the intolerable, the gradual acceptance of conditions that, if they had arrived suddenly rather than incrementally, would have produced an immediate and forceful collective response. We adapt, we cope, and we call it resilience when it might more accurately be called the attrition of expectation.

The Exhaustion Economy

The most pervasive symptom of ambient crisis, and perhaps the most revealing, is exhaustion. Not the healthy tiredness of productive work followed by rest, but a grinding, structural fatigue that appears to be affecting entire populations across developed economies simultaneously. It manifests as burnout rates approaching crisis levels in multiple professions. As sleep deprivation that has become so common it is treated as a personality trait rather than a health problem. As the epidemic levels of anxiety and depression that have been building for decades and accelerated sharply in recent years. As the widespread sense of being perpetually behind, unable to keep up, running to stay in place.

What is significant about this exhaustion is not its scale but its framing. The dominant cultural response has been to treat it as an individual problem requiring individual solutions, including better self-care, better time management, better boundaries, more resilience training, and more mindfulness. The system is not positioned as the problem. Your relationship to the system is the problem. Your inability to manage the demands of a system that was not designed with your wellbeing in mind is reframed as a personal failure of capacity. This framing is not incidental but functional, because it directs the energy that might otherwise be turned toward structural critique inward, toward self-improvement and self-blame. It transforms a social problem into a therapeutic one and sells the therapy back to the people the system has exhausted.

What is actually happening is more straightforward. The contemporary economy has, over several decades, systematically extended its claims on human time and attention while reducing what it offers in return. Jobs that require constant availability. Schedules that leave inadequate time for rest or relationship. Financial pressures that make any reduction in working hours feel too dangerous to risk. Digital technology that ensures work follows people into every space and every hour. The combined pressure runs at a level that human nervous systems were not designed to sustain indefinitely. This is not a metaphor. The neurobiology of chronic stress is well-documented, and sustained activation of the stress response degrades cognitive function, impairs immune function, disrupts sleep, damages cardiovascular health, and over time produces the psychological symptoms that we then treat as individual pathologies. The exhaustion is not a sign of personal weakness. It is the predictable physiological response to conditions that have been made progressively more demanding with progressively less recovery built in. When a system runs on depleting people faster than they can recover, it is not a sustainable system. It is extracting a resource it is not replacing, and the human consequences of that extraction, which show up in mental health data, in life expectancy statistics, and in the quiet desperation of people who are doing everything right and still falling behind, are the social equivalent of the ecological depletion described in the previous chapter. The mechanism is the same; only the resource differs.

Denial and Outrage

Psychologically, societies in decline tend to oscillate between two modes of response, and neither is particularly well-suited to the actual work of adaptation. The first mode is denial, which takes various forms: minimising the scale of problems, comparing unfavourably to worse situations elsewhere, appealing to historical hardship as a reason not to take current hardship seriously, or placing unconditional faith in future technological solutions. The common thread is the insistence that nothing fundamental is wrong, that concerns are overblown, that the current arrangement remains viable and preferable.

Denial is not simply irrational. Fully acknowledging systemic failure is cognitively and emotionally demanding, because it requires reconsidering things that have organised your life: career choices made in expectation of a stable system, beliefs about your society that have functioned as a form of identity, plans for the future premised on continuity. The psychological cost of that kind of revision is real, and denial is a defence mechanism, serving a genuine function even when it is also causing harm. Denial cannot be sustained indefinitely, however. Reality keeps introducing evidence that the workarounds are not working, that the adjustments are not sufficient, that the trajectory is not improving. When denial finally collapses, it tends not to give way gradually to clear-eyed assessment. It tends to flip, often quite suddenly, into outrage.

Outrage is the second mode, an intense focus on blame, on identifying who is responsible, on finding the scapegoat whose removal or punishment will restore what has been lost. It has the phenomenology of awakening, of finally seeing clearly after being deceived. It is frequently denial in a different register, however. The refusal to accept that the problems might be structural rather than personal, that solutions might require sustained collective effort rather than righteous indignation, that there may be no golden age to return to and no villain whose defeat would accomplish the return, is another form of avoidance. It allows for the emotional release of anger without requiring the harder work of understanding. Both modes are understandable. Neither is adequate. Denial prevents the adaptation that the situation requires, while outrage consumes the energy that adaptation would need. What the moment actually requires is harder to sustain and less emotionally satisfying: clear-eyed assessment of what is happening, honest acknowledgment of what has been lost and what is not coming back, and careful, patient thinking about what remains possible. That combination is rare in individuals and rarer in political cultures. It is, however, what distinguishes societies that navigate decline consciously from those that allow it to drive them toward authoritarian shortcuts.

Leaders Who Promise Restoration

Into the psychological volatility created by ambient crisis and the oscillation between denial and outrage steps a recognisable type of political figure: someone who promises simple solutions to structural problems, who offers restoration of a lost prosperity through force of will, and who provides the emotional satisfaction of a clear enemy to blame. This is a pattern so consistent across different historical periods and political systems that it amounts to something close to a predictable response to a predictable set of conditions. When societies experience decline that existing institutions are failing to address, when people are exhausted and frightened and the gap between official reassurances and lived experience has become too large to bridge, the appeal of someone who claims they alone understand the problem and alone have the will to fix it becomes genuinely powerful.

These leaders succeed not despite the implausibility of their promises but partly because of it. The very grandiosity of the claim, the suggestion that problems decades in the making can be resolved through sufficient political will, that the complexity can be cut through, that the enemy once identified and defeated will make things right again, is part of the appeal. It offers a way out of the unbearable combination of clear problems and unclear solutions. History provides no shortage of examples. Roman emperors who promised to restore Republican virtue while consolidating precisely the imperial power that had replaced it. Revolutionary leaders who promised liberation while building new forms of control. Nationalist politicians who promised to recover national greatness while the mechanisms they employed guaranteed further decline. The specific content differs across these cases, but the structure remains consistent: exploit genuine grievance, identify a legible scapegoat, promise restoration, concentrate power, fail to deliver, identify a new scapegoat, demand more power.

We are watching this pattern operate globally in the present moment. The appeal is real because the grievances are real. The political instability is not a product of manipulation alone. It is a product of the accumulated failure of existing systems to address the conditions that the previous three chapters have described: the exhaustion of the growth model, the dissolution of broadly shared prosperity, the normalisation of decline. Authoritarian promises gain traction when democratic institutions fail to deliver, and the failure is genuine, not merely perceived. The danger is not primarily that these leaders are unusually malevolent, though some are. The danger is that the solutions they offer are structurally incapable of addressing the problems they are responding to, while the methods they use to pursue those solutions tend to damage the institutional capacity that any genuine response would require. They are symptoms of systemic failure that, if acted on, tend to deepen it.

Recovery Begins with Relationships

History also consistently shows something that tends to receive less attention in accounts of collapse and decline, which is that recovery, when it comes, rarely begins with the right policy or the right leader or the right ideology. It begins with relationships. With people finding each other, recognising shared circumstances, building cooperative responses to conditions they cannot individually control. The formal systems having failed or retreated, the informal ones quietly expand to fill the space.

This is visible in the historical record with considerable consistency. After the collapse of Rome's western empire, it was monasteries and small communities, not any centralised political structure, that preserved knowledge, maintained agricultural practice, and provided the social stability from which later recovery became possible. After the Black Death, guilds and mutual aid organisations emerged to provide the protections that feudal arrangements no longer reliably offered. After the Great Depression, networks of mutual support, trade unions, and community organisations sustained people through circumstances that individual effort alone could not have managed. After acute disasters of every kind, the research literature on disaster response shows the same pattern, that the official response is slower and more cumbersome than the spontaneous cooperative response of people who find themselves in shared difficulty.

This is not romanticising hardship. These are responses to crisis rather than preferences. They reveal something important, however, about human capacity that the ideology of individual competition tends to obscure. We are a deeply social species, capable of remarkable cooperation under pressure, able to organise ourselves in the absence of, and sometimes in opposition to, formal authority. We can find genuine solidarity in shared difficulty, and that solidarity, the recognition that we are in this together and that what affects one of us affects all of us, is both more durable and more practically effective than it is usually given credit for. The question this raises is whether we can learn this lesson before crisis makes it mandatory rather than after, whether we can consciously rebuild the social fabric, the neighbour relationships and community institutions and mutual aid networks, that tend to dissolve during periods of growth and affluence and that tend to reconstitute themselves, painfully and slowly, after they have been lost. The social infrastructure that enables cooperative response to difficulty is much easier to maintain than to rebuild, and we have been allowing it to erode for a long time.

What We Practice Now

The psychiatrist and Holocaust survivor Viktor Frankl observed, from direct experience of conditions far more extreme than most of us will face, that what determined survival was not primarily the external conditions but the internal response to them. Not what happened to people, but the meaning they were able to make from it. The capacity to find purpose, to maintain connection, to act according to values even when the external reward for doing so was absent or negative, was not merely an admirable quality. It was a survival resource, with implications that extend beyond individual psychology.

We are entering a period of sustained difficulty. The ambient crisis is not resolving. The systems that produced the conditions described in this book are not reforming themselves at a rate that matches the urgency of the situation. More breakdown, more adaptation, more quiet attrition of what seemed fixed, is likely. In such a period, what people and communities practice now, in the years before the difficulties become undeniable rather than merely visible, will shape what emerges from them. The habits of solidarity or isolation, of honest assessment or motivated denial, of building something or simply protecting what you have, are not just private choices. They are, in aggregate, the material from which responses to collective difficulty are made.

If societies experience decline primarily through the lens of denial and outrage, through blame and division, through the search for strongmen to deliver simple solutions, then what emerges from the difficulty will reflect those responses: more authoritarian, more fragmented, more capable of violence and less capable of the sustained cooperation that genuine rebuilding requires. If they experience it instead through the harder combination of clear-sightedness and maintained solidarity, through honest acknowledgment of what is happening alongside the deliberate cultivation of the relationships and institutions that enable cooperative response, then something different becomes possible. Not guaranteed. Not inevitable. But possible in a way it would not otherwise be.

This is why the psychology of collapse matters, not as abstract knowledge but as a guide to practice. The choices available to us are not the grand political choices that dominate public discourse. They are, for most people in most circumstances, smaller and more immediate: whether to maintain connection or retreat into isolation, whether to acknowledge difficulty honestly or manage it through the comfortable fictions that denial provides, whether to invest in the relationships and communities around us or to treat social life as a cost to be minimised in favour of individual efficiency. These are not heroic choices. They are daily ones, and they are, cumulatively, the most significant ones available to most of us in the period we are living through.

Chapter Five

What Survives Every Time

When Systems Fail, Culture Endures

Travel to any region that experienced historical collapse and you will find something the standard narratives of decline tend to underemphasise. The systems that organised society, the governments, the economies, the formal institutions, are gone. The culture persists, however. The language, the stories, the music, the art, the ways people relate to each other and make meaning from their lives, all of these endure through centuries of political transformation and economic disruption, carrying something essential forward through conditions that destroyed almost everything else. This is not accidental. It reveals something fundamental about what human beings actually need, as distinct from what civilisations claim to provide.

We need food, shelter, and safety, which are material basics and are not negotiable. We also need meaning, connection, beauty, and the sense of belonging to something larger than ourselves, which are not luxuries appended to the material requirements once they are satisfied but requirements in their own right, without which the material ones become insufficient. Modern systems claim to provide both. Work provides income and purpose. Markets provide goods and the opportunity to acquire more of them. Government provides order and security. Technology provides connection and stimulation. The implied promise is that participation in the system will meet your needs, material and otherwise.

Systems are reasonably good at providing material goods, at least for those with sufficient purchasing power, and genuinely poor at providing meaning. Most modern systems actively undermine meaning by reducing everything to transaction, treating people as interchangeable units of production and consumption, optimising for metrics that have no connection to human flourishing, and demanding so much participation that people have little time or energy for the cultural practices that actually generate the meaning the system promises but cannot deliver. This is why collapse, paradoxically, sometimes increases human flourishing even as it reduces material abundance. When systems fail and can no longer extract all available time and energy, people remember how to be human. They make music. They tell stories. They help their neighbours. They gather and create and maintain the relationships that the system had been crowding out. After Rome's western empire fell, while material conditions declined, cultural productivity in many regions expanded: manuscripts were copied, new art forms emerged, oral traditions strengthened, communities organised around values that the imperial system had been too busy to cultivate. After colonial systems collapsed or retreated, Indigenous cultures across the world experienced renewals of language and practice that the colonial period had suppressed. After industrial economies contracted, community relationships that had been dissolving in the atomisation of consumer culture sometimes reconstituted themselves around shared circumstances.

The lesson is not that collapse is desirable. It is that systems and culture are different things, that material decline does not necessarily mean human decline, and that what survives the failure of formal institutions is often more valuable, more durable, and more genuinely human than what is lost.

The Things We Make That Make Us

Every human society creates art. Not as a surplus activity that occurs once survival is secured, but as a fundamental practice woven through the whole of life, the way we process experience, transmit knowledge across generations, build cohesion within communities, and make sense of existence at its most difficult and most beautiful. Consider music. Every culture produces it. Every historical period generates it. It survives when languages die, when religions transform, when political systems collapse entirely. Medieval plainchant is still performed. The spirituals created under slavery are still sung. Folk traditions persist across centuries, carried in memory and practice long after the conditions that produced them have changed beyond recognition. This persistence is not sentimental. It reflects something real about what music does that systems cannot, in that it creates shared emotional experience, enables collective processing of joy and grief, and binds people across time in a way that no institution can replicate.

Or consider story. The oldest preserved narratives in human literature, Gilgamesh, Homer, the epics and myths of cultures on every continent, are not instruction manuals or policy documents. They are explorations of what it means to be human, of how to face mortality, how to respond to suffering, how to find meaning in conditions that seem to resist it. They are cultural technologies for transmitting wisdom that cannot be codified in rules or reduced to advice, wisdom that must be encountered in the form of experience, even if that experience is imaginative rather than literal. Or consider the visual arts. Cave paintings made tens of thousands of years ago still move people who encounter them, and what was being communicated cannot be reduced to information. It was something closer to witness: this is what we saw, this is what mattered to us, this is what we want you to know existed. Every culture creates images for reasons that exceed recording and decoration. They are attempts to wrestle with questions that language approaches but cannot fully answer, including what is sacred, what is beautiful, what deserves to be remembered, and how we honour what matters.

These are not escapes from reality. They are engagements with reality at a depth that systems cannot reach. When economic systems fail, people still need to process grief. When political systems fail, people still need to imagine alternatives. When the institutions that were supposed to provide meaning fail to do so, people still need to find or create it. Art, in its broadest sense, is how we do that, and the evidence of history is that we do it regardless of whether circumstances are favourable, often most urgently when they are not. What this means for our moment is that as systems fail to deliver on their promises, as material conditions contract in some domains while expanding in others, as institutions lose legitimacy and coherence, culture becomes more important rather than less. The things we make together, the art, music, story, and ritual that cannot be purchased or manufactured at scale, will matter more than the things we buy separately, and the capacity to create and share meaning will be more valuable than the capacity to accumulate. This is not hopeful rhetoric. It is historical observation.

The Imagination Is the Last Thing They Can Take

Václav Havel, the Czech playwright who became his country's first post-communist president, wrote with unusual precision about what had sustained dissidents through decades of oppression under a system that controlled nearly every material aspect of their lives. It was not, he argued, hope in the conventional sense, the expectation that the system would change or that their efforts would succeed, because that kind of hope was difficult to sustain against the evidence available to them. What sustained them was something both simpler and more durable, the conviction that maintaining human dignity and creativity mattered regardless of outcome, that totalitarian systems could control behaviour and resources and movement but could not fully colonise consciousness, that the imagination remained free even when the body was constrained.

This is a precise and important observation. Systems can control resources. They can mandate participation and punish noncompliance. They can shape what people are able to do with enormous effectiveness. They cannot fully control, however, what people think, what they value, or what they create in the spaces that are not monitored and the moments that cannot be regulated. The imagination, which is to say the capacity to envision something other than what currently exists, is the one resource that cannot be entirely expropriated. This is why authoritarian systems treat culture as a security threat, why the control of art, literature, music, and public speech is always among the first priorities of governments moving toward totalitarianism, why banning books, censoring music, and persecuting writers and artists is not an incidental feature of authoritarian rule but a structural one. Culture is where people maintain the capacity to imagine alternatives, where values that systems cannot co-opt are preserved and transmitted, where the memory that things have been different and therefore could be different again is kept alive.

Imagination is remarkably resilient. Banned books circulate in secret. Forbidden music is sung quietly. Dissident art finds the cracks in whatever system is trying to suppress it. The human capacity to create meaning, to maintain hope not as passive expectation but as active practice, has persisted under conditions that should by any material calculation have extinguished it. People who lose the capacity to imagine alternatives to degrading conditions internalise those conditions as natural and inevitable. They stop being able to see them as constructed, contingent, and therefore changeable. People who maintain imaginative capacity, whatever their material circumstances, retain the ability to recognise that current conditions are not permanent facts about reality but choices that were made and could in principle be unmade. They can act, now, according to values they want to see embodied later. They can build, in small and mostly unrecognised ways, the world they are working toward. The question is not whether imagination is practical, then, but whether survival without it is recognisably human.

The Ritual Economy

Every known human culture practises ritual, formal and informal practices that mark time, create meaning, bind communities, and affirm values that are otherwise abstract and invisible. The evidence for this is so universal and so ancient that it is difficult to interpret it as anything other than a fundamental feature of human social life rather than a cultural preference. Modernity has been somewhat hostile to ritual in its traditional forms, associating ceremony and tradition with superstition and irrationality, and the premise was that rational, scientifically informed people could organise their lives without the scaffolding of inherited practice. The evidence has not been kind to this premise. The decline of traditional rituals did not produce communities of rational individuals who had transcended the need for collective meaning-making. It produced communities in which the ritual impulse was redirected toward whatever structures were available, including sports events, consumer holidays, brand loyalty, and the ceremonial practices of digital life. The need did not disappear. It was captured by forms that serve commercial and corporate interests rather than community ones.

What anthropological research consistently shows is that ritual, in its authentic form, does something that cannot be replicated by other means. It creates social reality rather than just reflecting it. Marking a transition through ceremony makes it real in a way that the mere passage of time does not. Gathering regularly with a community, performing shared practices, creates the social bonds that those gatherings are sometimes assumed to merely express. Treating certain times and places as set apart from the ordinary, as worthy of a different quality of attention, produces a different quality of experience that has measurable effects on wellbeing and social cohesion.

During periods of institutional failure and social fragmentation, the resurgence of informal ritual is one of the most consistent patterns in the historical record. After acute disasters, communities create memorial practices spontaneously, before any official response has organised. During the disruptions of recent years, people invented new ways of marking time and maintaining connection in the absence of the usual structures. When formal institutions fail to provide the meaning and belonging they once organised, informal rituals emerge to fill the space, usually less perfectly, always more honestly. What this suggests for the period ahead is that investing in the ritual life of communities, the regular gatherings, the shared practices, the deliberate marking of transitions and seasons and losses and celebrations, is not a luxury to be deferred until material conditions improve. It is part of the infrastructure of resilience. Communities with strong ritual life are better able to absorb difficulty, maintain cohesion under pressure, and recover from disruption, and the practices that seem optional are often the ones that matter most when conditions become testing.

The Remnant That Remembers

In every historical collapse, among all the loss and disorder, there are people who make a different choice, who consciously preserve what they recognise as worth preserving: the knowledge, the practices, the values, the memory of how things worked and what they were for. The monks copying manuscripts in the early medieval period were not powerful figures in the world they inhabited. They were often marginal, sometimes persecuted, rarely celebrated in their own time. What they were doing was recognised as important only much later, when it became clear that the texts they had copied were among the main channels through which the intellectual achievements of the ancient world had survived to become available again. Indigenous communities maintaining languages and traditions through centuries of colonial suppression were performing a similar act of stewardship, keeping alive the knowledge and identity that colonialism was trying to extinguish, making possible the cultural renewals that would come later. Archivists preserving records during wars, teachers maintaining standards during institutional collapse, doctors and nurses maintaining professional ethics under systems that reward otherwise: these are all versions of the same practice.

The writer Rebecca Solnit has described what she calls an invisible community of stewards, people who maintain parks and public spaces, preserve traditions and knowledge, protect vulnerable populations, document what is actually happening rather than what the official narrative claims, teach carefully and honestly, and build things meant to last rather than to impress, knowing their work will not be celebrated and may not be recognised but is nonetheless essential to whatever comes after. The temptation during periods of decline is cynicism. If the system is broken, why maintain anything? If the institutions are corrupt, why uphold standards they routinely violate? If the future is uncertain, why sacrifice present advantage for a future that may not come?

The answer is both practical and philosophical. Practically, cynicism and opportunism in crisis compound the crisis, because the scramble for individual advantage at the expense of collective welfare is exactly the dynamic that makes collective recovery harder. Every person who maintains honesty in a culture of dishonesty, or care in a culture of extraction, or long-term thinking in a culture of short-term calculation, is doing something that has disproportionate effect on the social environment around them. The remnant that remembers does not stop the collapse, but it determines what is available to build from when the collapse has run its course. Philosophically, the question of what kind of person to be does not wait for better conditions. It is answered, always, by what is done now, in the conditions that actually exist. The values we want to see in the world are either practised or they are not. The knowledge and practices worth preserving are either maintained or they are lost. The bridge between what was valuable in the past and what will be needed in the future is built, person by person, in the ordinary decisions of ordinary lives.

What Survives, and What We Are Building

We are living simultaneously in late-stage decline and early-stage emergence. The old system is failing across multiple domains. New forms of organisation, new practices, new relationships between people and communities and the natural world, are developing in the spaces the failing system is vacating. Both processes are real. Both are continuing. The disorientation this produces is itself a feature of transition: we want clear narratives in which either everything is fine or everything is catastrophic, and the reality stubbornly refuses either simplification.

What history shows, with unusual consistency across very different times and places, is that what survives collapse is not what was most powerful or most prominent in the preceding system. It is what was most deeply human. The music. The stories. The relationships. The knowledge held in practice rather than in institutions. The values maintained by the remnant that remembered them when remembering was costly and unrewarded. This has an implication that is both clarifying and demanding. It means that the work that matters most in the period of transition, the work that will determine the character of what emerges, is not primarily political or economic or technological, though all of those matter. It is cultural, in the broadest sense, the work of maintaining and creating the human things that systems cannot provide and cannot destroy.

Hope, in this context, is not optimism. Optimism is the expectation that things will work out well, and it is fragile, because it depends on conditions remaining favourable enough to sustain the expectation. Hope is something different and more durable. It is the determination to act meaningfully regardless of whether things work out well. It does not require a favourable assessment of the odds. It requires only the conviction that acting according to values matters in itself, that building small goods is worthwhile even when large structures are failing, that the attempt to remain human in dehumanising conditions is worth making even without guarantee of success. This is the hope that sustained people through the plagues and wars and depressions and exiles that fill the historical record, not the belief that everything would be fine but the conviction that maintaining humanity through crisis was worthwhile whether or not the crisis resolved, that what we do in the difficult time shapes what becomes possible in the time after it, that the world being built, in the ruins and around the edges of the collapsing one, is being built by people who refused to accept that the collapsing one was all there was or ever could be.

We are those people, or we can choose to be. The question is not whether circumstances are propitious, because they rarely have been for most people in most times. The question is what we are making, maintaining, and protecting in the time that is available to us, what we are building in the space between the end of one way of organising the world and the beginning of whatever comes next. The answer to that question is not written in advance. It is being written now, in the ordinary decisions of ordinary lives, in ways that will only become fully legible to people who come after us and inherit what we have left them. What we want that inheritance to contain is the question this chapter has been moving toward, and it is the question each of us answers, day by day, in the choices that determine what survives our particular passage through the long unravelling.

Chapter Six

How to Live in the Long Unravelling

The Question the History Can't Answer

The five preceding chapters have been diagnostic. They have traced how progress became theology and why that theology is now producing diminishing returns. They have followed the arithmetic of infinite growth to its physical limits. They have examined the historical accident of the middle class and the political consequences of its dissolution. They have described the psychology of living through decline without recognising it as such. And they have looked at what, in every previous collapse, has survived: the cultural, relational, and imaginative resources that systems can neither fully provide nor fully destroy. A careful reader might reasonably ask, and so?

The history is illuminating, and the patterns are clear, but pattern recognition alone does not tell you how to live. It does not tell you what to do with the clarity once you have it, how to hold the knowledge of structural failure without either being paralysed by it or becoming so accustomed to crisis that you stop feeling the urgency of what is actually happening. It does not tell you how to maintain your humanity inside systems designed to extract it, how to find meaning in circumstances that are not of your choosing, or how to act with integrity in a period when the institutions that are supposed to model and reward integrity are visibly failing to do so. History can show you the pattern. It cannot tell you how to be a person inside it. That is what this chapter attempts, not as a list of prescriptions, because the diversity of circumstances people occupy makes prescriptions almost always false in someone's specific situation, but as a set of hard-won recognitions drawn from both historical observation and the considerable body of knowledge we have accumulated about how human beings actually function under sustained difficulty. The aim is not to make the long unravelling comfortable. It is to make it navigable.

Begin with What Is Actually Happening

The first and in some ways most demanding task is simply to see clearly, which sounds easier than it is. As Chapter Four described, the dominant psychological response to systemic failure is oscillation between denial and outrage, and neither mode allows for the clear-eyed assessment that navigation requires. Denial refuses to acknowledge the scale of what is actually happening, while outrage acknowledges it but channels the energy into blame, which is emotionally satisfying and practically limited. Both modes are understandable, and neither is particularly useful as a basis for living well.

What clear seeing requires is something that does not come naturally in conditions of chronic stress: the willingness to hold difficulty without immediately either minimising it or catastrophising it. To say that this is genuinely hard, and it is also not the end of everything, and both of those things are true simultaneously. The difficulty is real, and the capacity to navigate it is also real, with neither claim cancelling the other. This kind of seeing is not a personality trait but a practice, and like all practices it is developed through repetition rather than through inspiration. It involves, in concrete terms, regularly distinguishing between what you actually know, what you are inferring, and what you are fearing, three categories that are easily and constantly conflated in conditions of ambient anxiety. The situation is genuinely difficult. The specific trajectory it will take is uncertain. The worst-case scenarios that anxiety generates are real possibilities but not certainties. Keeping these categories separate does not eliminate the difficulty. It makes it possible to respond to what is actually there rather than to the catastrophised version that anxiety tends to produce.

There is a clinical term for the capacity to hold difficult realities without being overwhelmed by them: distress tolerance. It is not the same as acceptance, which implies agreement, and it is not the same as resignation, which implies abandoning effort. It is the capacity to remain functional and responsive in the presence of realities that cannot be immediately resolved, which is precisely the capacity that a long-term structural transition requires. The historical figures who navigated periods of collapse most effectively were not those who were most optimistic, and not those who were most alarmed. They were those who were most accurate, who saw the situation as it was, without the distortion of either wishful thinking or catastrophic imagination, and who acted from that accurate perception rather than from a managed or distorted version of it.

Distinguish What You Can Influence from What You Cannot

The Stoic philosophers, who developed their thinking in conditions of political instability and personal vulnerability that were in some respects not unlike our own, made a central distinction between what lies within our power and what lies outside it. They were not the first to make this distinction, and they were not the last. Nearly every serious tradition of thought about how to live under difficult circumstances arrives at some version of it.

The distinction is not between the important and the trivial. The things outside our individual power include some of the most important things, including the structural forces driving inequality, the political choices that will determine how the climate transition unfolds, and the trajectory of democratic institutions under authoritarian pressure. These matter enormously, and they are also not, for most people in most circumstances, directly within individual control. Confusing what matters with what we can individually control is one of the most reliable sources of the combination of grandiosity and despair that characterises a particular kind of political engagement, the sense that you must personally fix everything, followed by the collapse into paralysis when it becomes clear that you cannot. The grandiosity and the despair are two sides of the same misunderstanding.

What individuals can influence, in most circumstances, includes a narrower but not insignificant set of things: the quality of attention they bring to their immediate relationships, the values they act on in their daily work, the community they participate in or help to build, the honesty of their engagement with what is actually happening, the practices they maintain or let slide, the people they choose to support or become. This is not a counsel of passivity. Collective action, which has driven every significant progressive change in the historical record, is made up of individual decisions to participate, to show up, to contribute time and attention and effort to something larger than private interest. The individual contribution is not nothing, but it is one contribution among many, and the clarity that comes from understanding it as such, neither more nor less than what it is, is both more accurate and more sustainable than the alternative.

There is a practical implication here that is easy to state and difficult to live by: concentrate your energy where you can actually make a difference, not where the problem is largest but where your particular combination of capacities, relationships, and circumstances gives you genuine leverage. The scale of a contribution matters less than its reality. Small genuine goods, done consistently and with care, compound over time in ways that are difficult to see in the moment and significant in the aggregate.

Take the Long View, and Also the Short One

One of the characteristic distortions of living through a period of rapid change is temporal, the tendency to collapse everything into either the immediate present or the indefinite future, losing the middle ground where most actual living occurs. The immediate present is urgent. The news cycle, the political developments, the economic pressures, the social crises, all of these demand constant attention and produce a state of perpetual reactivity that is both exhausting and, over time, cognitively narrowing. People living in a state of chronic reactivity lose the capacity to think in longer timeframes, to notice patterns that only become visible over years rather than days, to sustain commitments that take time to bear fruit. The indefinite future presents its own distortions. Climate change, civilisational transition, the question of what the world will look like for people who are children now, these are genuinely long-term concerns that deserve serious attention. When they function primarily as sources of anxiety about an imagined future rather than as guides to present action, however, they consume the energy that present action requires without contributing anything to it.

The historical perspective that runs through this book is useful precisely because it occupies a middle temporal register, longer than the news cycle and shorter than geological time. It is a perspective that can see patterns developing over decades and centuries without losing sight of the human scale at which those patterns are lived, and it consistently shows that the people who navigated transition most effectively were those who could hold both timeframes simultaneously, the long view that provided context and direction and the short view that determined what to actually do today.

In practical terms, this means maintaining commitments and practices that operate on a longer timescale than crisis allows. The relationship built over years. The skill developed through sustained practice. The institution maintained through consistent contribution even when it seems to make no immediate difference. The child raised with enough security and honest attention to develop genuine resilience. These are long-game investments, and they matter more, over time, than any equivalent expenditure of energy on reactive responses to immediate crises, however urgent those crises genuinely are. It also means, paradoxically, taking the present seriously enough not to lose it to anxiety about the future. The moment of genuine connection with another person. The work done well for its own sake. The experience of beauty or meaning or rest that is available now and will not wait for better conditions. These are not distractions from the serious business of navigating difficult times. They are, partly, what the navigation is for.

Invest in Relationships as Infrastructure

Chapter Four argued that recovery from collapse begins not with policy or ideology but with relationships, and this chapter needs to say something more specific about what that means in practice and why it is not simply an appeal to interpersonal warmth.

Relationships are infrastructure in a precise and non-metaphorical sense. They are the channels through which information, resources, care, and practical assistance flow in conditions of difficulty. The research on how communities respond to acute disasters consistently shows that the most important variable in determining outcomes is not the quality of official response, though that matters, but the density and quality of existing social connections. People with strong networks of genuine relationship are better able to obtain help, provide it, coordinate action, share accurate information, and maintain the psychological stability that continued functioning requires. The infrastructure of relationship is what makes collective response to difficulty possible at all.

This infrastructure takes time to build and is easily neglected during periods of relative affluence, when it seems less immediately necessary. The atomisation that characterises contemporary life in many developed societies, the decline of shared institutions, the physical design of suburbs that discourages encounter, the replacement of community participation with digital connection, the busyness that crowds out the time that genuine relationship requires, has been quietly degrading this infrastructure for decades. We are now in a period when we need it more and have less of it than at any previous point in living memory for many communities.

Investing in relationships as infrastructure means treating the time and attention that genuine relationship requires not as a discretionary expenditure competing with more productive uses of time, but as a fundamental investment in resilience. It means prioritising depth over breadth, since a small number of genuine relationships in which honesty, mutual support, and real knowledge of each other's circumstances are possible is more valuable, as infrastructure, than a large number of superficial connections. It means showing up consistently rather than intensively, since relationships are built through the accumulation of ordinary interactions rather than through occasional significant ones. And it means investing in the shared institutions, the local organisations, the community groups, the neighbourhood connections, through which individual relationships aggregate into something with collective capacity. None of this requires exceptional social skill or unusual generosity. It requires primarily time, attention, and the willingness to prioritise something whose returns are not immediately legible in the metrics that contemporary culture uses to measure a well-spent life.

Find the Work That Is Yours to Do

One of the most demoralising features of living through systemic crisis is the scale disproportion between the problems and the individual. Climate change, democratic backsliding, economic inequality, the erosion of social cohesion, all of these are civilisational-scale challenges, while the individual confronting them is, materially, almost negligible in scale. The gap between the magnitude of the problem and the magnitude of the individual contribution available can produce a kind of paralysis: why do anything, given how much needs to be done and how little any one person can accomplish?

The historical record offers a useful corrective. The changes that matter most in retrospect are almost never produced by a small number of exceptional individuals acting on a civilisational scale. They are produced by large numbers of ordinary people doing specific, local, particular things, including teaching, organising, building, creating, maintaining, caring, documenting, and resisting in the modest ways available to them. The abolition of slavery was not the project of a handful of heroes. It was the accumulated effort of thousands of people over more than a century, most of whom are not remembered individually and did not live to see the outcome of their work. The same is true of every significant progressive change in the historical record. The scale at which the change eventually operated was built from contributions at a much smaller scale, most of which seemed, at the time, inadequate to the problem.

What this suggests is that the useful question is not how to solve the civilisational problem, which is not a question that can be answered at the individual level. The useful question is what particular work, in the specific circumstances of your particular life, is yours to do. What capacities do you have that are relevant to what is needed? What relationships give you access to places where genuine contribution is possible? What do you see that others are not seeing and that needs to be said? What do you know how to do that could be used in service of something larger than private interest?

The answers to these questions will be different for everyone. For some people the work is explicitly political: organising, advocacy, building the institutions through which collective power can be exercised. For others it is cultural: making, teaching, preserving, creating the art and story and ritual through which communities maintain their identity and transmit their values. For others it is relational: the sustained care of particular people, the maintenance of particular relationships, the building of the community fabric that everything else depends on. For others it is economic: building organisations that operate according to different values, demonstrating that alternatives to extractive practice are viable. None of these is more important than the others, and none of them is sufficient alone. What matters is that the work is genuine, that it is actually done rather than merely intended, that it connects to real circumstances rather than to an imagined heroic role, and that it is sustained over time rather than performed in bursts of inspired energy followed by periods of exhausted withdrawal.

The historian who has shaped my own thinking on this more than any other is not one of the canonical names of the discipline. It is the unnamed ones: the archivists, the teachers, the community organisers, the people who showed up when showing up was unrewarded and whose contributions only became visible later, when what they had maintained turned out to be exactly what was needed. They did not know they would matter. They did what was in front of them to do, with the capacities they had, in the circumstances they actually occupied, and that, in the end, is the only standard available to any of us.

On Grief, and Why It Is Not the Enemy

Something that serious writing about systemic crisis often omits, perhaps out of concern about overwhelming the reader, is the emotional reality of what it means to understand what is being lost.

The middle class that the previous generation experienced as simply normal is dissolving. The ecological stability that has underlain agricultural civilisation for ten thousand years is being disrupted at a rate that has no precedent in human history. The institutional frameworks, the democratic norms and the regulatory systems and the social contracts, that previous generations built at significant cost and that provided the conditions for the broadly shared prosperity of the mid-twentieth century are being dismantled, partly through neglect and partly through deliberate effort. The assumption that the future would resemble the past closely enough for the same maps to work is no longer reliable. These are genuine losses, and they deserve to be grieved. Not wallowed in, not used as permission for despair or passivity, but genuinely felt, because the things being lost were genuinely worth having and the people who are losing them are genuinely affected.

There is a clinical and experiential observation that is relevant here, which is that grief that is not allowed expression tends not to disappear but to find other outlets, usually less productive ones. The rage and despair and cynicism that characterise significant portions of the contemporary political landscape are in part expressions of unmourned loss, loss of security, of expectation, of the sense that the world is organised in ways that bear some relationship to fairness. When loss cannot be named as loss, when the cultural message is relentless forward momentum and the acknowledgment of what has been lost is framed as weakness or sentimentality, the grief goes underground and resurfaces as something harder to work with.

Allowing grief its proper place is not in tension with the kind of clear-sightedness and purposeful action that this chapter is arguing for. It is a precondition of it. People who are not allowed to mourn what has been lost cannot accurately assess what remains. They are working with a distorted picture of their actual situation. The person who can say honestly that this has been lost, that it mattered, that they are sorry it is gone, and that here is what they are going to do with what remains, is better positioned for the work ahead than either the person who pretends the loss did not occur or the person who is so overwhelmed by it that they cannot act. The losses of the long unravelling are real, and they do not require minimising. What they require is the kind of honest acknowledgment that makes it possible to also see what has not been lost, what remains, and what might yet be built.

What Clarity Is Actually For

This book began with a simple observation, that every civilisation believes it is permanent until it is not, and that the people living through decline experience it not as catastrophe but as ordinary life. The purpose of the historical lens this book has offered is to interrupt that ordinariness enough to see it for what it is. Not to produce panic, which is neither useful nor historically warranted. Not to produce despair, which is a kind of luxury that the circumstances do not really allow. But to produce the clarity that makes genuine response possible rather than merely reactive.

Clarity about what is happening is a resource. It does not make difficult things less difficult, but it makes them navigable in a way that denial and confusion do not. It allows you to distinguish between what is actually threatening and what is merely uncomfortable, between what requires immediate response and what requires patient sustained effort, between what is within your sphere of influence and what requires collective rather than individual action. These distinctions matter enormously for how energy is spent and whether that spending produces results.

The historical record, read honestly, is neither reassuring nor devastating. It shows that civilisational transitions are genuinely difficult, that they produce real suffering, that the outcomes are not predetermined and depend significantly on choices made by people living through them. It also shows that human beings have navigated such transitions before, that what is most valuable in human culture has consistently survived conditions far worse than those we currently face, and that the capacity for cooperation, creativity, and the making of meaning has proved more resilient than any particular system that claimed to be the only framework within which those things were possible. This is not a promise that things will be fine. It is something more useful, the evidence that things have been as difficult as this before, and that people found ways to live through it with their humanity intact, and sometimes to build from what remained something worth the building.

That is what the long unravelling asks of us. Not heroism, not certainty, not the resolution of problems whose resolution is not within individual reach. It asks for clear seeing, honest acknowledgment, the patient cultivation of the relationships and practices that make human life worth living, and the willingness to do the particular work that is ours to do, without requiring that we be able to see, from where we are standing, how it will all come out. History never offers that kind of reassurance. What it offers is something else, the evidence that it has been done before, that people who had far less clarity than we do, far fewer resources and far worse odds, still managed to maintain enough of what mattered to make the future possible, and that we have available to us, in the conditions we actually occupy, at least that much.

CONCLUSION

The Pattern and the Possibility

We began with a simple observation, that every civilisation believes it is permanent until it isn't, and that the people living through its decline experience it not as catastrophe but as the accumulation of ordinary days. Six chapters later, that observation has been examined from multiple directions. We have traced how progress becomes theology and why the theology eventually produces the conditions for its own failure. We have followed the arithmetic of infinite growth to its physical limits and watched it turn, when those limits press, into the financialisation and speculation that concentrate wealth without creating it. We have examined the middle class as a historical accident rather than a natural feature of capitalism, and the political consequences that reliably follow when the conditions that produced it are dismantled. We have described the psychology of living through decline without recognising it as such, the shifting baselines, the ambient exhaustion, the oscillation between denial and outrage that prevents the clear-eyed adaptation the situation requires. We have looked at what survives in every collapse, the cultural, relational, and imaginative resources that systems can neither fully provide nor fully destroy. And we have tried to say something honest about what it means to live well inside all of this, not by escaping the long unravelling but by navigating it with clarity, with sustained relationship, with grief where grief is warranted, and with the particular work that each person's circumstances make available to them.

The pattern is clear. We have been here before, in different forms, under different names, but following dynamics consistent enough to be studied and understood, and that consistency is the reason this book exists. It is not offered as prophecy or as comfort. It is offered as orientation, the kind of perspective that becomes possible when you can see your own moment from outside it, even partially, even imperfectly.

What the historical lens reveals is that we are not exempt from the forces that have shaped every previous civilisation. Our technological sophistication does not make us immune to civilisational cycles. Our economic frameworks do not exempt us from physical limits. Our democratic institutions, valuable as they are and worth defending, do not automatically protect us from the political instability that extreme inequality reliably generates. We are living through a genuine transition, not a temporary disruption that will resolve itself back into the familiar, and the pattern is visible to anyone willing to look at it directly. The historical lens also reveals something that straight-line extrapolation from current trends tends to miss, however. Transitions of this kind, however difficult, have been navigated before. Not always well. Not without enormous suffering. Not without loss that was irreversible and grief that was legitimate. But navigated, in the sense that human communities came through them, carrying enough of what mattered to make something from what remained. The monasteries that preserved classical knowledge through the contraction of the early medieval period did not know they were doing something historically significant. The mutual aid networks that sustained communities through the Depression did not know they were demonstrating a model that would prove essential later. The dissidents who maintained honest witness under totalitarian systems did not know which of them would live to see those systems fall. They did what was in front of them to do, with the capacities they had, in the circumstances they actually occupied.

This is the historical evidence that matters most for the present moment. Not the specific outcomes, which were various and contingent, but the consistent finding that what determined those outcomes was less the scale of the structural forces at work and more the quality of response available from the people living through them: whether communities had strong enough social fabric to support cooperation under pressure, whether enough people maintained the practices and values worth preserving to make them available for rebuilding, whether the cultural resources, the art and story and ritual and memory, were kept alive through the difficult period, whether those navigating the transition could see it clearly enough to respond to what was actually happening rather than to denial or outrage. These are not factors outside individual influence. They are, in aggregate, made up of individual decisions: to maintain relationship or retreat from it, to act honestly or conveniently, to invest in the slow work of community or to concentrate entirely on private security, to preserve what is worth preserving or to let it go in the general erosion.

None of this is a guarantee. History is not deterministic. The future remains genuinely uncertain, and anyone who tells you otherwise with confidence is selling something. The long unravelling may produce outcomes far worse than anything the historical parallel suggests, or far better, or some mixture of both in different places and different domains simultaneously. What individuals and communities do in this period will influence those outcomes, but it will not determine them alone. Structural forces operate at a scale that exceeds individual action, and collective choices, made through institutions and political processes and cultural shifts that aggregate millions of individual decisions, will matter more than any single contribution. What individuals can do is contribute honestly to those aggregates, which means, in practice, seeing clearly rather than conveniently, maintaining relationships that have genuine depth rather than performing connection, doing the particular work that is yours to do rather than waiting for conditions to be more favourable, allowing grief its proper place rather than converting it into something harder to work with, and keeping alive, in whatever sphere of life you actually inhabit, the practices and values and imaginative capacity that the longer pattern of human history suggests are worth keeping.

This is both less and more than the grand historical agency that people sometimes fantasise about. Less, because it does not involve directing the course of civilisation or resolving problems of civilisational scale. More, because it is actually available, to most people, in the circumstances they actually occupy, without requiring exceptional resources or extraordinary courage or historical good fortune.

The cycle we are in is old. The dynamics have been observed before, by people who studied them with the tools available to them and tried to understand what they meant, and we have the advantage of their observations, accumulated across thousands of years and dozens of civilisations, which is an advantage that no previous generation has had in quite this form. We can see the pattern. We know something about what follows from it. We know something about what has helped and what has not, about what survives and what tends not to, about the kinds of response that make the difference between navigating a transition and simply being carried by it. Whether we use that knowledge is a question that the history cannot answer for us. It can only show us what is at stake in the answering.

The future is still being written. It is being written now, in the choices that people make about how to live and work and relate to each other in the middle of a transition that most of them experience, on any given Tuesday, as simply ordinary life. That is where all the large historical shifts have always been made, in the ordinary life of people who were living through something they did not yet have a name for. We have a name for it, which is not nothing, and what we do with the clarity is the question that remains, in the end, the only one that matters.

Notes

The Long Unravelling draws on a wide range of historical, economic, and psychological scholarship. Rather than interrupting the prose with numbered citations, the works most directly informing each chapter are listed below, organised by chapter, with brief contextual commentary where it serves the reader. Those wishing to explore the wider literature will find the Further Reading section that follows organised by theme rather than by chapter, which allows for deeper engagement with whichever strand most resonates.

Introduction

The framing of historical patterns and the discussion of how civilisations experience their own decline draw most directly on Joseph Tainter's *The Collapse of Complex Societies* (1988), which remains the standard scholarly treatment of systemic decline and the diminishing returns of complexity. Barbara Tuchman's *The March of Folly* (1984) is the indispensable companion volume on the psychology of why states so consistently pursue policies against their own interest. The systems-modelling perspective that informs the book's overall argument originates with Donella Meadows et al., *The Limits to Growth* (1972), and Karl Polanyi's *The Great*

Transformation (1944) provides the foundational analysis of how market systems and the societies that contain them shape one another over time.

Chapter One: When Progress Becomes Religion

The treatment of how growth assumptions become embedded in the institutions and imagination of a society draws on Meadows et al., *The Limits to Growth* (1972), and on John Maynard Keynes' essay "Economic Possibilities for our Grandchildren" (1930), which remains the most useful early statement of the question of what economic activity is actually for. Frederick Jackson Turner's "The Significance of the Frontier in American History" (1893) is the original analysis of the frontier as a defining feature of American development. E. P. Thompson's *The Making of the English Working Class* (1963) informs the social history of industrialisation. Naomi Klein's *The Shock Doctrine* (2007) provides context for how progress theology has been deployed politically in recent decades, and Polanyi's *Great Transformation* remains the underlying analytical frame.

Chapter Two: The Fallacy of Infinite Growth

William Stanley Jevons' *The Coal Question* (1865) is the original source for what is now called Jevons' Paradox. Meadows et al., *Limits to Growth* (1972), provides the systems-dynamics modelling. Tim Jackson's *Prosperity Without Growth* (2009) and Kate Raworth's *Doughnut Economics* (2017) are the most accessible contemporary statements of post-growth economic frameworks. Herman Daly's *Beyond Growth* (1996) develops the steady-state economics tradition. Vaclav Smil's *Energy and Civilization* (2017) is the definitive work on the material and energetic basis of economic activity. Compensation data referenced in the chapter is drawn from the Economic Policy Institute's CEO Compensation reports (2020 and subsequent).

Chapter Three: The Middle Class Mirage

Claudia Goldin and Robert Margo's paper "The Great Compression" (1992) is the original economic-history treatment of the mid-twentieth-century narrowing of inequality. Thomas Piketty's *Capital in the Twenty-First Century* (2013) provides the longest-run data on wealth concentration in market economies. The Economic Policy Institute's *State of Working America* (various years) supplies the productivity-and-wage data discussed in the chapter. Robert Putnam's *Our Kids: The American Dream in Crisis* (2015) examines the dissolution of social mobility, and Arlie Hochschild's *Strangers in Their Own Land* (2016) is the most empathetic ethnography of communities affected by industrial decline. Polanyi's *Great Transformation* remains essential, and Jacob Hacker and Paul Pierson's *Winner-Take-All Politics* (2010) traces the political choices that produced the inequality returns of the past forty years.

Chapter Four: The Psychology of Collapse

Viktor Frankl's *Man's Search for Meaning* (1946) is the foundational text on meaning-making under extreme conditions, and his observations inform the chapter throughout. Daniel Kahneman's *Thinking, Fast and Slow* (2011) provides the cognitive-science background for how people process slow-developing threats. Rebecca Solnit's *A Paradise Built in Hell* (2009) is the essential work on how communities respond to acute disaster, contradicting the popular assumption of social breakdown. Naomi Klein's *Shock Doctrine* (2007) provides parallel analysis of how political opportunists exploit such moments. Robert Putnam's *Bowling Alone* (2000) documents the long erosion of civic infrastructure. Bessel van der Kolk's *The Body Keeps the Score* (2014) supplies the neurobiology of chronic stress that underlies the chapter's treatment of structural exhaustion. The concept of shifting baseline syndrome originates with Daniel Pauly's "Anecdotes and the Shifting Baseline Syndrome of Fisheries" (1995).

Chapter Five: What Survives Every Time

Václav Havel's essay "The Power of the Powerless" (1978) is the central text on dissident culture and the survival of imagination under totalitarian conditions. Rebecca Solnit's *A Paradise Built in Hell* (2009) again provides indispensable evidence on community resilience. Victor Turner's *The Ritual Process* (1969) supplies the anthropological framework for understanding ritual as social technology. Robin Wall Kimmerer's *Braiding Sweetgrass* (2013) shapes the chapter's treatment of cultural continuity and indigenous knowledge traditions. Lewis Hyde's *The Gift: Imagination and the Erotic Life of Property* (1983) informs the discussion of culture as gift economy. Ursula K. Le Guin's essay "The Carrier Bag Theory of Fiction" (1986) reframes the act of storytelling itself.

Chapter Six: How to Live in the Long Unravelling

The Stoic distinction between what is within our power and what is not draws on Epictetus' *Enchiridion* (c. 125 CE). Viktor Frankl's *Man's Search for Meaning* (1946) returns as a central reference. Elizabeth Kübler-Ross's *On Death and Dying* (1969) supplies the framework for the chapter's treatment of grief as necessary rather than indulgent. Joanna Macy and Molly Young Brown's *Coming Back to Life* (1998) develops the practice of allowing grief in service of meaningful action. Adrienne Maree Brown's *Emergent Strategy* (2017) shapes the discussion of working at scale through relationship and small consistent actions. Rebecca Solnit's *Hope in the Dark* (2004) is the most useful contemporary essay on the difference between hope and optimism. The research on disaster response and social capital draws on Daniel Aldrich's *Building Resilience* (2012).

Further Reading

The works listed below extend the major themes of *The Long Unravelling*. They are grouped by subject rather than by chapter, on the assumption that readers will follow the threads that most engage them rather than the structure of any single book.

History and Civilisational Cycles

Joseph Tainter, *The Collapse of Complex Societies* (1988). The essential scholarly account of systemic decline.

Barbara Tuchman, *The March of Folly* (1984). On the recurring tendency of states to pursue policies against their own interest, with case studies from Troy to Vietnam.

Jared Diamond, *Collapse: How Societies Choose to Fail or Succeed* (2005). Comparative environmental and political histories of decline.

Peter Turchin, *War and Peace and War* (2006). On the structural cycles that produce political instability across very different civilisations.

Karl Polanyi, *The Great Transformation* (1944). The foundational analysis of how market systems and the societies containing them shape one another, and what happens when the relationship breaks.

Simon Schama, *Citizens: A Chronicle of the French Revolution* (1989). On how an apparently stable order can come undone, told at the human scale of those living through it.

Economics, Limits, and Alternative Frameworks

Donella Meadows et al., *The Limits to Growth* (1972). The original systems-dynamics modelling of finite-planet constraints, more accurate in retrospect than its critics allowed.

Tim Jackson, *Prosperity Without Growth* (2009). The most accessible contemporary statement of post-growth economic possibility.

Kate Raworth, *Doughnut Economics* (2017). A reframing of economic goals around social foundations and ecological ceilings, increasingly influential in policy circles.

Thomas Piketty, *Capital in the Twenty-First Century* (2013). The most thorough long-run data on wealth concentration under market capitalism.

Herman Daly, *Beyond Growth* (1996). The classic statement of steady-state economics by its most rigorous theorist.

Mariana Mazzucato, *The Value of Everything* (2018). On the difference between value creation and value extraction in contemporary capitalism.

Vaclav Smil, *Energy and Civilization* (2017). The definitive work on the material and energetic foundations of modern economic life.

Psychology, Meaning, and Living Through Difficulty

Viktor Frankl, *Man's Search for Meaning* (1946). The foundational text on meaning-making under extreme conditions, still indispensable nearly eighty years on.

Bessel van der Kolk, *The Body Keeps the Score* (2014). The contemporary standard on the neurobiology of trauma and chronic stress.

Rebecca Solnit, *A Paradise Built in Hell* (2009). On how communities actually respond to disaster, against the popular assumption of breakdown.

Joanna Macy and Molly Young Brown, *Coming Back to Life* (1998). On the relationship between grief and meaningful action.

Adrienne Maree Brown, *Emergent Strategy* (2017). On working for change at scale through relationship, attention, and small consistent practice.

Robert Putnam, *Bowling Alone* (2000). The long documentation of civic erosion in late-twentieth-century America.

Daniel Kahneman, *Thinking, Fast and Slow* (2011). On the cognitive architecture that makes systemic threats so difficult to process.

Culture, Imagination, and What Survives

Václav Havel, *Open Letters: Selected Writings 1965–1990* (1991). The essential collection from one of the great dissident essayists, including "The Power of the Powerless."

Rebecca Solnit, *Hope in the Dark* (2004). The most useful contemporary essay on hope as practice rather than optimism.

Robin Wall Kimmerer, *Braiding Sweetgrass* (2013). On the survival and transmission of cultural and ecological knowledge across centuries of suppression.

Ursula K. Le Guin, *The Wave in the Mind: Talks and Essays on the Writer, the Reader, and the Imagination* (2004). On story, language, and what they do that systems cannot.

Lewis Hyde, *The Gift: Imagination and the Erotic Life of Property* (1983). On creativity as gift economy, and what is lost when culture becomes commodity.

Victor Turner, *The Ritual Process* (1969). The anthropological account of ritual as social technology.

Marilynne Robinson, *The Death of Adam* (1998). Essays on what has been lost in modern thought and what might be recovered.

About the Author

Racquel Hines Lynch writes at the intersection of economics, history, and psychology. Her work explores how these three forces shape the lives of individuals and societies in turbulent times, and how we might respond to them with clearer thinking and more humanity.

She publishes the weekly essay *Time's Mirror* on Substack, where she examines historical patterns, economic and systemic analysis, and the psychology of living through difficult moments. Her readers are based across Australia, Canada, the United States, and beyond.

She lives and writes in Australia.

The Long Unravelling is her first book.

For more of her work, visit rhlwrites.com.

www.ingramcontent.com/pod-product-compliance
Lightning Source LLC
LaVergne TN
LVHW100332210926
848480LV00003B/1318
9781764771405